POSITIONAL PLAY

Strikers

by
Allen Wade

Published by
REEDSWAIN INC

Library of Congress Cataloging - in - Publication Data

Wade, Allen
  Positional Play - Strikers

ISBN No. 1-890946-08-7
Copyright © 1997 Allen Wade
Library of Congress Catalog Card Number 97-075739

Reedswain books are available at special discounts for bulk purchase. For details contact the Special Sales Manager at Reedswain 1-800-331-5191.

Credits: Art Direction, Layout, Design and Diagrams • Kimberly N. Bender
Cover Photo: Empics

REEDSWAIN VIDEOS AND BOOKS, INC.
612 Pughtown Road • Spring City Pennsylvania 19475
1-800-331-5191

Table of Contents

ii

Chapter 1
The Striker's Role and Responsibilities in Team Play

T he two players whose roles have changed least of all in modern soccer are the goalkeeper and the striker. Although his role may not have changed much, the striker's style of play has altered in keeping with the varied and variable strategical and tactical attitudes demanded by top class competition.

Nevertheless, strikers remain specialists. . . at least outstanding strikers do. They have capabilities for scoring goals, for putting the finishing touches to attacking play, which appear to be 'natural' gifts rather than merely learned skills. In fact all of a striker's skills can be learned and practiced in exactly the same way as those of other players.

Genius in soccer, like genius everywhere is, as Edison said, "One percent inspiration and ninety nine percent perspiration". → Sweat

High class modern soccer requires all out-field players to develop a range of techniques and tactical skills which will enable them to defend or to attack as any situation demands.

Any of the backs and all of the mid-field players will find themselves in shooting positions from time to time. Nevertheless, a good team. . . certainly a great one. . . will have one or more players with the 'special' skills needed to score consistently when lesser players, in identical shooting situations, will be much less certain.

Before we can examine how the best strikers actually play, we need to do a job analysis on the striker. We need to identify his special role in team play, his specific responsibilities and those attributes which are vital to success in forward play.

The striker's team role is:

1.1   To score goals and to dominate those areas near to goal from which most goals are scored.

1.2   To disturb and to set problems for defenders in such ways as to make it easier for teammate to score.

1.3   To link together the various players available to take part in attacking play.

1.4   To lead attacking play positively, with optimism and enthusiasm. When his team is under the most severe pressure he. . . often alone . . . must offer them outlets and hope; the hope that something can be created out of nothing.

1.5 To deflect and contain attacking moves by opposing backs, always acknowledging his primary priorities as attack leader. A striker who, within reason, accepts his share of the hard running and challenging which defensive play involves, is an inspiration to his team.

The great Hungarian teams of the early nineteen fifties played to an unwritten rule that any player who lost the ball had to work the hardest to get it back. All their world class forwards, Kocsis, Czibor, Puskas and the great Nandor Hideguti, their invisible man, had to sweat with the rest.

Chapter 2
Responsibilities

From the definition of his role, the responsibilities of the striker fall into place logically.

2.1 He must be inside or close to the penalty area, preferably close to the goal area, whenever there is the likelihood of the ball arriving.

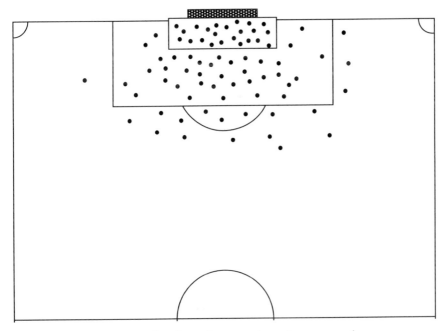

Diagram 1. *Scattergram showing where most goals are scored.*

In diagram 1, the 'scatter' shows the places from which goals are scored in top class soccer. The nearer to the central goal area the greater the number of goals scored, the further away the fewer.

The majority of goals are not scored from clearly worked and cleverly created shooting opportunities. Most are scored as a result of deflections, rebounds, balls dropped by the goalkeeper, defenders' mis-kicks and similar 'lucky' or 'unlucky' occurrences.

Great strikers live in a state of permanent certainty that, by luck or by good judgment, the ball **WILL** arrive at their feet, one way or another.

They are not concerned with how stylish the goal looks, only with putting the ball into the net. This gives them the incomparable advantage over other players of always being prepared, mentally and physically, for its arrival.

2.2 The striker must be prepared to struggle, or to use any sort of trickery, within the laws, to get to the ball first. Being first to the ball, with head or foot. . or any other part of his body allowed by the laws, is fundamental to being an effective striker. Whenever the ball is in the penalty area or close to it, the striker must position himself so that when the ball comes, his body position and the position of his feet will allow him to assume an effective shooting 'shape'.

2.3 The striker must 'show' himself intelligently for any kind of passes from his own defending players.

He will be the furthest and most attractive outlet for defenders who are under severe pressure. He must develop an acute sense of possibility and of need. If he senses that his defense is under severe or growing pressure, he must guarantee a safe outlet for them.

A guaranteed outlet for passes encourages defenders to 'play out' with optimum control rather than merely kicking the ball desperately up field. At the same time it allows them to regain composure and time to move into mutually supportive positions.

Defenders under siege are reluctant to move out at all: they only want a respite. . . any sort of respite. . . from attacking pressure.

2.4 All good strikers must be capable of receiving and holding the ball to give supporting players time to move within easy range of return passes. He must be the ultimate link with all players moving to attack.

To achieve this, a striker must be prepared to accept severe pressure from opponents, even physical intimidation, while maintaining the highest possible levels of composed skill.

2.5 A striker has important space controlling responsibilities.

Often he is tightly marked by one opponent who is closely covered by another. The striker's movements therefore affect the space occupied by three players. More than any other player, he can cause space to be highly congested or he can free it.

WHERE space should be made available, **WHEN** it should be made available and **HOW** strikers can set about freeing it, make up the tactical skills which strikers must develop. We shall discuss those later.

2.6 Strikers must take advantage of every opportunity to ⬛ behind or to the side of defenders.

However, when making forward runs, if they over-stretch ⬛ between themselves and supporting players, they will find them ⬛ off and isolated.

If they begin their runs too soon they may move beyond the rang ⬛ the passing player's skill and power. The run will be a waste of effort a ⬛ the pass will be intercepted.

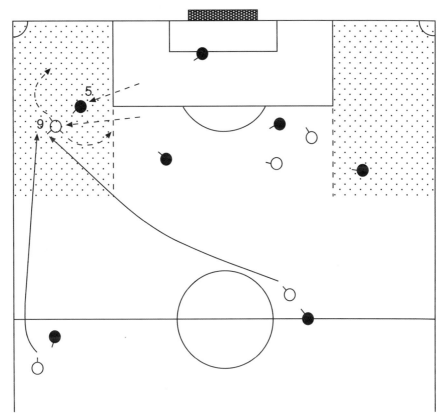

Diagram 2. *Exploiting the wide channels (shaded).*

Occasionally a striker will invite a forward pass, particularly into the wide channels, diagram 2, where he can screen (shield) the ball and turn past his marker or hold it and wait for the arrival of supporting attackers.

Knowing WHEN, WHERE AND HOW to create space for himself or for other players is one of the hallmarks of a great soccer player.

2.7 Strikers, stationed centrally for much of the time, can affect the relationship between all the opposing backs and often between the backs and defending mid-field players as well.

t outside the penalty area and restricted to the
th, will be a cause of concern to all defenders.
that a pass will not reach the striker; they can
vill be unable to shoot; they are never certain
anyway. It may be to create a shooting chance
a chance for another attacker.
is to be answered at once, often in a split second,
comfortable for defenders.
y the quickest thinkers on a soccer pitch: I know, I was
of the action for long periods, they don't get enough practice. Making opponents think quicker than they enjoy is an important skill
and the striker is the player best positioned of all to do it.

2.8 Attack is, often but not always, the best form of defense.

When it is elaborately developed in a team's own half of the pitch, it encourages early aggressive defending. Risks taken to regain possession of the ball before it is transferred over the half way line are worthwhile.

As 'first' defenders, strikers have important responsibilities for containing and deflecting the threat of effective attacking play among the opposing backs and through mid-field.

Front players must compel or persuade opponents to move the ball into areas of the pitch which are likely to be least damaging to their own mid-field and back players, all of whom will be re-organizing in defense.

Strikers, who are unwilling to work to contain opposing backs and to make their play more predictable, are dangerous. . . to their own team!

The role of a striker as outlined here, together with his responsibilities, provides a logical basis for deciding which tactical skills he needs most. In turn, these tactical priorities determine what the range of his techniques must be. Finally, these tactical and technical 'needs' will determine the content and the intensity of the players' training and practice programs.

However, the younger the players the greater the need for emphasis on their development as all-round players, capable of playing competently and skillfully in any position.

Specialist inclinations, such as exceptional shooting skills or extraordinary dribbling ability, should be encouraged but not at the expense of extending the players' experience in all playing positions. Early specialization in this position or that may produce ego massaging results for managers and coaches: it will do nothing for players other than inflate their expectations of success to unreasonable levels.

Chapter 3
The Principal Attributes of
High Quality Strikers

S uccessful teams in modern soccer are based upon a large number of all around players, sometimes to the exclusion of positional specialists. At the highest levels of soccer, players are expected to play comfortably and competently in all or most out-field positions and outstandingly well in one or two.

Modern defensive strategies and tactics, involving high degrees of organization and discipline, ensure that this trend will continue.

Fluid interchanges of position in which responsible, individual initiatives are encouraged, are the means by which defensive strangulation will be defeated. African countries, not yet contaminated by tactical paralysis and the fear of losing, still produce players with the skill and ingenuity to play to win. . . for the time being.

Forward thinking teams are developing strategies within which players move into and out of attacking and scoring positions from all parts of the pitch.

Mobility is the way to stretch rigid marking and covering deployments to the breaking point. However, mobility alone will be of minimal value if players lack the techniques, in quality, range, and cunning, to enable them to function effectively as all round players.

Some players will continue to develop specialized positional play. Early success can be so highly rewarding that the urge to pursue special positional skills will never change. A lasting commitment to the game, in a special way, may spring from early worship of a particular soccer hero. Imitation of that player's attributes may become all consuming and achieved at levels simply unattainable by less powerfully 'driven' players. Strikers possess that special magnetism.

Before proceeding may I make plain my commitment to the totality of the soccer player. Often for the purpose of study and analysis we pigeon hole aspects of human performance; we separate and label them. We talk about physical attributes as if they are separable from, and independent of, psychological considerations.

The fact of course is that any condition of the mind has significant and increasingly better understood effects upon the performances of our bodies and conversely, physical well being has a comparable effect upon our mental attitudes. For my purposes here, I may refer to attributes as physical, physiological or psychological, so that what I have to say may be more clearly understood by soccer players and coaches. I accept that the interdependence of human characteristics is complete and their effects absolutely complementary.

3.1 Goal Obsession.

Scoring goals is as much an attitude of mind as it is a skill. Some would have us believe that great scoring ability is instinctive, something which a player simply has or does not have. That is nonsense. Goal scoring is learned and therefore it can be taught. All players can become significantly better through intelligent teaching and imaginative practices; all will enjoy the experience.

Learning to strike a ball accurately past a goalkeeper into a target area eight yards wide and eight feet high presents few problems until a player is expected to do so, every time, in front of a hundred or a hundred thousand spectators. Great strikers have a kind of tunnel vision when it comes to shooting and scoring: until that moment they are often normal players. All of them have highly developed perceptions of where the goal is, where the goalkeeper is within it, what he is doing, what the probability is of the ball arriving and how it may arrive, what the likelihood is of opponents interfering with the shooting opportunity and so on. They have a capacity for programming all this information simultaneously before executing a difficult contact with the ball at precisely the right moment in precisely the right way. All of this can be learned and taught.

Strikers are possessed by a hunger for goals and are prepared to prowl, patiently and alertly in those areas from which their hunger may be satisfied. It is a fact of soccer life that more goals are scored within or near to the goal area than from anywhere else within the penalty area. The implications are obvious, 'be where action pays off'. Some strikers want to play as modified, advanced mid-field players. They seek every opportunity to drop deep to link up with support players; they are adept at laying off passes; they join in neat interpassing movements with anyone and everyone and they even score well struck goals from impressive distances. . . occasionally.

Often, they are pretenders seeking to delegate the responsibility for scoring.

Real strikers just score. . . often!

3.2 Tough Mindedness.

Call it what you will, determination, competitiveness, tenacity, never giving in if you like. The sheer will power to get to the ball first is vital to any striker.

Good ones have this attribute in abundance, even at the risk of personal injury. They share it with those with whom they are often in direct confrontation, goalkeepers. Both must get to the ball first.

In professional soccer, defenders set out to test the determination of strikers early in the game. Anything and everything may be tried, legal and otherwise. . . especially otherwise. They talk to him, stare him down, touch him, hold him, tread on him, not to mention intimidatory tackling. They may succeed in making the opponent angry but great strikers don't get angry, they only get even. Shrewd defenders set out to create discord between opposing attackers. They encourage the moaner, the striker who always blames his bad luck or the bad play of teammates for his own failures, by sympathizing with him. 'Professional' defenders are trouble seekers and makers; breaking an opponent's concentration is their business. Strikers have to develop immunity to this sort of treatment by building up steely, unshakable determination. It has to be learned and can be taught.

3.3 Courage.

Courage may involve determination but it isn't the same thing. Courage may be 'physical' in that a player may go through with an action which he knows is likely to be painful. To head the ball just as an opponent is about to kick it requires courage. The player knows what is likely to happen but does it anyway. But courage may be moral; an action may have no physical consequence at all. This is the courage required to accept personal responsibility for an action when failure could be absolutely final and could affect every other member of the team. A striker who chooses to shoot when a pass would transfer the ball and shift the responsibility is courageous. To take a penalty kick when a miss might cost his team huge rewards, even a place in the game's history books, requires considerable moral courage. Strikers must be willing to shoot and to take the responsibility for missing.

3.4 Composure.

Strikers, the game's stars and heroes, live in the game's limelight. Some revel in acclaim others are unmoved by it. The former are self orientated, they want to win for themselves first and the team second: the latter the other way round.

They are the players likely to appreciate the finer points of striking skills and also the difficulties which have to be overcome. Both types of player are highly successful although idolized players sometimes have difficulties coping with their successes. They may believe that they are bigger than the team or the game itself. They lose the calculating composure upon which a striker's skill depends and, when things go against them, they look in every direction other than inwards for the cause of and the solution to problems. They can be educated to modify their behavior.

Strikers need the composure to change their perspectives during a game. They need to stand outside the game to assess opponents' play: to calculate their technical strengths and limitations: to judge their agility and speed: to assess their opponents' thought processes. Strikers must be capable of thinking ahead or of reacting to situations as and when they occur. This ability to look on the game as an outsider requires out of the ordinary composure. A striker, out of the game for substantial periods, must have the composure and the concentration to be always in it mentally. Composure gives a striker the edge when, inside the penalty area with the ball, he coolly sends a lunging defender the wrong way, fakes a shot causing the goalkeeper to take off in a despairing dive and calmly rolls the ball into the opposite corner of the goal.

It is, I believe, known as staying cool!

3.5 Persistence.

Strikers are required, often, to take up the same positions over and over again, even when the arrival of a pass seems barely conceivable. Teammates under pressure need to know where exactly relief is certain to be. Certain positions in different phases of play will be vital to team tactics. Tactics succeed or fail by the extent to which all players understand in principle and accept what they are all trying to achieve. This is not to say that each player must do this or that, the game cannot be played according to statistical precognition. It is to say that within certain agreed possibilities each player will try to exercise his skill accordingly. This becomes the game 'sense' which some players seem to be born with and which enables them to move apparently intuitively into effective positions. The sense isn't intuitive, it is learned although often untaught.

Effective strikers always make themselves available to teammates, however intimidating the circumstances. Some have the supreme skill of invisibility to opponents but they always reappear where they are most wanted for their own players. Strikers high in persistence compel opponents, especially markers, to worry about what they are up to. And they don't have to be physically busy to do so, until they need to be.

Top strikers worry defenders most when they are doing nothing.

3.6 Visibility.

Mention has been made of the need for a striker to be 'seeable' by his own players: being seen doesn't mean being heard!

Of all the players, strikers should be seen but rarely . . . I never say never

. . . heard! They, Strikers, must be visible as much as possible in and near to the penalty area but being visible doesn't mean being magnetic, he shouldn't be a compulsive target for all players with the ball. Strikers, as we have seen, have important responsibilities for making space and scoring opportunities for others. Visibility in attacking situations is often directly related to a striker's accessibility: often but not always. Subtle strikers show themselves for obvious passes (but don't want them) when alternative pass receivers might be better bets.

3.7 Mobility.

The best strikers are more often than not restlessly on the move although not necessarily at speed. They 'prowl' in search of the ball or for positions in which they can embarrass opponents, but never at the expense of losing contact with supporting players. By frequent, sometimes constant movement they cause defenders to move when those players would pre-fer to remain in the organized, highly integrated, positional relationships upon which so much of modern defensive play is based. In fact it is the degree of organization and integration in defensive commitments which frequently has such a negative effect upon a team's attacking play. Totally reliant upon a system, the likelihood of quick, voluntary switches into imaginative, surprising play is minimal.

Players on the move first, however low their speed, will always win races for position or for the ball; the shorter the race the more certain the result. For strikers, mobility is infinitely more important than size. Size in a striker invites limited methods of exploitation. The heads of exceptionally tall players or very high jumpers become obsessive targets for all other players: advantage becomes handicap. Play becomes unimaginative and tactically sterile.

If a striker has exceptional speed teammates may over emphasize urgent, long passes, often too soon, too long and hopelessly inaccurate. Assets become liabilities. Given an outstanding attribute a team should minimize its employment. Opponents, nervously aware of an opponent's special attribute, will never be sure where or when he will bring it into play.

Nervous defenders are vulnerable defenders.

An unwarranted belief in the need for tall strikers has been one factor which held English soccer back for more than thirty years. In most profes-sional clubs the belief continues.

Tactical sterility is a consequence of deficient mobility.

3.8 Touch.

Passing the ball, stopping it, kicking it long or short, heading it and even shooting to score with precisely the amount of 'weight' needed is another hallmark of quality players. They have no need for violence towards opponents or to the ball. Violence is an excessive use of force and in a game designed for supreme human skill it is unnecessary.

A striker's receiving touch of the ball may be his only touch. He operates in the smallest of spaces and under the intimidating influence of one or two opponents. Space equals time in soccer. If a player has enough time to do what he chooses to do clearly he has enough space. The ability to direct the ball precisely, with a single touch, with any part of his anatomy, is of paramount importance to any player with higher aspirations: especially to strikers. Strikers, sooner or later, must learn to do whatever is necessary with the fewest of touches: eventually with only one, at the most two. Young players of course must be concerned with accurate ball contacts and controlling movements before concentrating on single ball contacts. Nevertheless they should be made aware that the higher the class to which they aspire the less the time and the fewer the touches available to use their various skills. A striker with excellent touch is hard to handle because he never shows a defender enough of the ball to invite a legal challenge. Good touch players are extremely dangerous inside penalty areas because illegal challenges invite serious punishments.

Most international teams in modern times have chosen mobile, touch players before soccer light houses. Gorillas have been replaced by guerrillas.

From time to time of course, players with exceptional physical attributes will emerge and will change the direction, momentarily, of the game's tactical development. They should not however change the principles of attack in which mobility is an important consideration.

3.9 Acceleration.

Acceleration is not speed, it is change of speed. There are players with exceptional speed who need time in which to accelerate. Acceleration, in soccer, is not so much a matter of achieving a certain speed, it is the quality necessary to change pace smoothly and thereby deceptively. Strictly speaking this attribute should be headed 'acceleration and deceleration'. A striker who can 'change gears' effortlessly, up and down, doesn't need to accelerate to high speed. In fact high speed soccer players often seek to use their speed too often. Deception, when moving for or with the ball is achieved by subtle changes of speed. Relatively slow players, in straight track sprinting, can develop change of pace. First, they will have to develop variations in body language. Players need to learn how to appear to be running much faster than they actually are.

Running speed is achieved by the force exerted on the ground by the feet (thrust) and by the number of times over any given distance that the thrust is exerted effectively. A third and related factor is the length of each stride.

Apparent muscular tension, facial expression, height of knee pick up and so on may be associated with sprinting hard in the minds of observers but if they don't reflect the principles stated earlier they are of little relevance. If, while applying the three principles to optimum effect, a player can achieve an air of casual relaxation in his general appearance and effortlessness in his limb movements, he is likely to seem to be running a good deal slower than is actually the case. A small lengthening of the stride with no appreciable change in stride pattern increases speed apparently effortlessly. A player looking about him while sprinting, whether with a good reason for doing so or not, gives a deceptive air of less than maximum effort when he may be moving almost as fast as he can. (Soccer skills, as they are applied at the top level, depend for deception upon uses of the body and the limbs in such ways as to hide real intentions) Soccer players' body languages may be fluent but they are likely to be deceitful.

3.10 Vision.
. . . and good eye sight is only half of it. Many soccer players have 20:20 eye sight and no vision to speak of. (A striker's vision is the ability to see and remember what is happening and what seems likely to happen in even the remotest parts of the pitch.) How and where different players are moving: at what speed and if possible to judge, why? To what extent are any players free from markers or from cover? Is the opposing defense balanced or do the backs take risks by lying square? Where if anywhere are possible spaces or holes in defense which might be exploited? Great soccer players see all that they need to see and most of what their teammates should see as well. Strikers also have finely developed sight lines from their feet or heads into goal. They can visualize shooting opportunities where lesser players wouldn't know where to look.

No matter how long a good striker is out of the immediate action his visual perception should have been trained to enable him to see and interpret all the clues leading to profitable interplay. Vision will come from carefully designed practice situations which make progressively more difficult demands upon perception. We still have a lot to learn about learning in soccer.

Chapter 4

The Striker's Playing Environment

Before identifying the personal tactical skills which are important foundations of a striker's success, we should examine the various situations in which he has to play: his playing environment if you like. This will give us a realistic idea of the striker's special problems and, for coaches, a basis for designing effective practice situations.

(a) He plays facing his own goal for much of the time.

(b) He is marked 'touch-tight' whenever and wherever the ball is likely to come to him.

He may be tightly marked even when he is unlikely to receive a pass.

(c) The player marking him is likely to be covered closely by another defender.

(d) Marked and covered tightly, the striker may have to find ways of contributing to his team's play without actually getting the ball.

(e) There may be a 'picket' player patrolling the area in front of him, diagram 3.

(f) When he turns with the ball, often he will be tackled vigorously and, if he is a skillful turner, perhaps late.

(g) When receiving the ball, under severe pressure from opponents, the striker will have a split second in which to decide what to do. Frequently, having decided what to do, he will have to change his mind.

(h) A striker may be out of the game for long periods when his team is defending; his concentration will be severely tested.

(i) When opportunities occur, a striker must have retained the alertness and concentration to take them; they don't come too often!

(j) Under considerable pressure, teammates may deliver badly directed and poorly weighted passes to him; he will be expected to make something out of anything.

(k) In shooting situations, the ball may arrive unpredictably; the striker has to be first to it with whatever part of his body happens to be most convenient.

The ideal of scoring from a composed, inter-passing move or from a beautifully executed, flying, gymnastic movement is fine. . . as an ideal. Most goals are scored from goalmouth scrambles which depend more

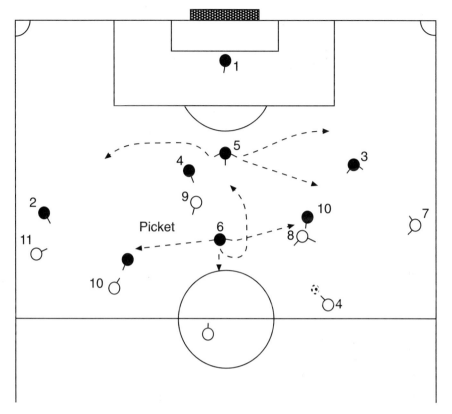

Diagram 3. *The defensive picket blocking access to strikers.*

upon alertness, forcefulness and persistence than upon precise skill.

Opponents will be equally intent upon getting to the ball and with similar force and determination.

To re-emphasize an important point, goal scoring is as much a matter of attitude as of technical skill.

All of the previous conditions affect the striker's function and consequently the tactics and techniques he needs to be successful.

Chapter 5
Tactical Skills

Personal tactical skills are the methods and tricks used by one player, with or without the ball, to gain advantage over opponents. They allow a player to set problems for opponents for which there are often two or more answers, only one of which is the right one. The problems require an opponent to decide WHAT he should do, HOW he should do it and most difficult of all, WHERE and WHEN.

A striker's personal tactical skills will be needed according to the situations in which he finds himself. These occur as follows:

5.1 In and close to the opponents' penalty area
5.11 with the ball or receiving it.
5.12 without the ball.

5.11 In and close to the opponents' penalty area, with the ball or receiving it, the striker's action options are to:
- hold the ball and work for a chance to pass or shoot.
- make an immediate pass to another attacker.
- shoot with the first touch of the ball.
- 'fix' a marker
- turn and shoot with two or more touches.
- 'fake' a shot and pass or 'fake' a pass and shoot.
- draw opponents away from good defending positions.

Other options will be variations but from these we can identify the required tactical skills.

5.111 Holding and Hiding the Ball.

To receive and hold the ball close to or inside the penalty area, while tightly marked and covered, the striker must receive the ball sideways on to his marker. The whole width of his body and the spread of his legs keeps the marker as far from the ball as possible.

Strikers must know the passing capabilities and have a good idea of the usual intentions of the pass deliverers. Usually the pass into or near to the penalty area must travel between or over opponents. The greater the distance between the passer and the space between defenders, the harder the ball must be hit and the greater the controlling problem for the receiver, diagram 4.

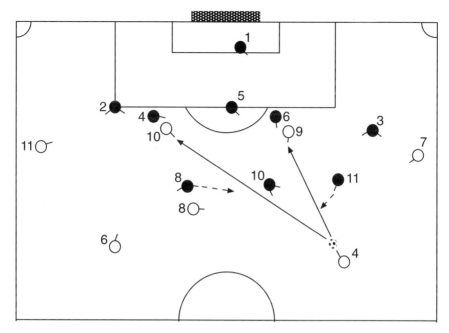

Diagram 4. *Passing through the first defensive curtain.*

The greater the distance, the greater the likelihood of the gap being closed and the pass intercepted.

The passer must hide his intentions while measuring the gap, judging the distance involved while assessing the target player's movements.

The striker must appreciate the passer's problems.

If the striker moves into position too soon, his marker may intercept the pass or direct co-defenders to tighten up and narrow the gap.

The striker must hold a position away from the gap or make a 'fake' move in another direction before moving into a receiving position as late as possible. Diagram 5.

Late, quick movements by strikers generate quicker responses from defenders. Defenders forced to move quickly can be 'turned' more easily than those moving to suit themselves. The striker's late move into position should give him three action options. . . to hold the ball, to pass or to turn and shoot.

'Fake' moves are essential for success. He may 'fake' to pass but turn, or 'fake' to turn but pass. In other words he must learn to be a 'con' man: to build up the confidence of opponents and trick them. 'Fake' moves are the foundation of the soccer 'con' man's art.

Screening (hiding) the ball while receiving is easier if the striker can move into a position as tight as possible against his marker and between

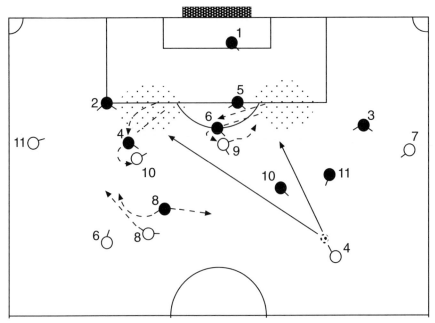

Diagram 5. *Passing through first defensive curtain clearing space for the re-entry.*

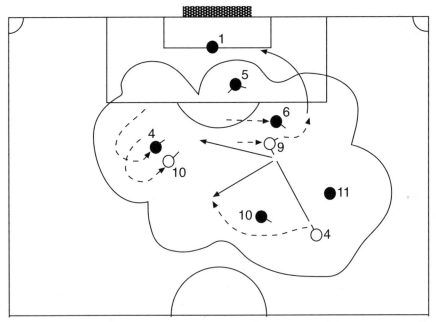

Diagram 6. *Laying off passes into space left by an attacker's movement.*

him and the oncoming ball. The closer together the players are the more difficult it is for the marker to see the ball or tackle for it legally.

If the defender moves to the side of the striker, to see the ball better or to intercept, the striker can 'spin off' him in the opposite direction.

The closer they are, the more the striker can use his body to keep the opponent away from the ball. As he rolls around and away from his marker, the striker is facing goal. It will be almost impossible for the defender to make a recovery tackle without committing a foul.

This 'spin-off' move is almost unstoppable if the passing player follows his pass close to or beyond the striker.

This supporting move gives the striker a dangerous passing option and opponents will not be sure which move to counter, the spin-off or the pass to the supporting player.

5.112 Instant Passing.

A first time pass, particularly where the passer 'lays the ball off' in a surprising direction, can create good shooting opportunities for alert supporting players.

In a situation similar to that in 5.111, the striker moves into position behind the gap and deflects a pass back into the space from which he started his run. Diagram 6. The passing player, following his own pass, veers away at the last moment towards the space which the striker left and into which he has deflected the ball.

Experienced defenders know that a skillful attacker only needs a quarter turn to left or right to enable him to achieve a reasonable shooting position.

The defender's first duty is to prevent or to block the shot on goal.

In diagram 6, the striker is moving to receive a pass slightly to one side of the goal and he is 'shaping' to turn and shoot with an 'outside' turn i.e. a turn away from his marker. To block a shot, the defender must move from a marking position between the striker and goal, i.e. an 'inside' position, to a position where he, the defender, is slightly outside that line. Diagram 6.

If the striker can deliver an inside pass, while faking an outside turn and shot, the pass will be difficult to stop by the central marker.

A supporting player, moving with determination into the space vacated by the striker, is likely to have the time and the room to release his shot.

To move or not to move, that is the question. . . for all attackers inside the penalty area. Some strikers in the penalty area move too often and too quickly. Moving too often alerts defenders. Moving quickly makes receiving the ball that much more difficult.

Inside the penalty area strikers can be dangerous when they stand still, or when they move relatively slowly over short distances. . . **AT THE**

RIGHT TIME.

By standing still, especially close to an opponent, they 'fix' him.

Here the most effective first-time pass from the striker may be a pass 'laid back' towards the player who played it into the penalty area in the first place, or to another supporting player along the same line. This return pass must be 'short' to enable the supporting player to move in to shoot from as close to goal as possible.

5.113 First Time Shooting.

First time shooting serves two purposes, to make sure of a shot at goal and to persuade defenders that the striker is likely to shoot first time **EVERY TIME!**

When defenders expect shots they tend to relax. Once the shot has been made defenders know that it is up to the goalkeeper. Shooting first time from unlikely scoring positions occasionally may 'con' nearby defenders into relaxing. When the next opportunity occurs, the striker can 'fake' a shot and turn to lay-off a pass or shoot, following a second or even a third touch. With doubts planted in his mind, the defender may be poorly prepared to do anything about it.

Alternatively, passes laid off can be used to 'set' up defenders for the first time, surprise shot.

Successful soccer is a matter of bluff and double bluff.

Successful first-time shooting is a matter first of attitude and second of technique. Technical skills will be dealt with later, in detail.

Attitude reflects the determination of the striker to steal away from or in front of defenders to be first to the ball. Where the striker gains some space and time, he sets himself for the shot by 'seeing the body shape' he will have to assume to contact the ball accurately through the 'line' to the target.

5.114 'Fixing' an Opponent.

Many strikers make the mistake of always trying to move away from their markers when the arrival of the ball is imminent.

Presumably they imagine that defenders cannot read the passer's intentions. Unfortunately good defenders can: to intercept passes they have to!

Standing still or moving comfortably makes receiving a pass easier. Marking and covering players follow the movement patterns of the players they are marking, at least until the ball is on its way.

At the highest level, a striker will find little time and space in which to prepare himself for a shot: often none at all.

A striker must learn to make the most of simply getting his foot or his head. . . or anything. . . to the ball first. Sometimes it hurts!

Occasionally, <u>clever strikers stay close to their markers</u>. Both will know where the ball is targeted as soon as the passer has hit it . . . perhaps even sooner. The striker only needs a split second in which to throw a fake move to 'con' his marker into believing that he has read the situation better or differently.

<u>By creating the smallest of doubts in the defender's mind he 'sets the defender up' to be beaten in the race for first contact with the ball.</u>

Markers who have 'tunnel' vision and only concentrate on the behavior of the player they are marking are often the easiest to beat.

Marking can be too tight for comfort. . . for the comfort of the marker that is!

5.115 Shooting on the Turn.

With his back towards goal, hitting a shot early and on target is a matter of making a quarter or a half turn before the ball arrives. If the striker needs to play the ball twice before shooting, almost certainly the second touch will be a fake shot. The first touch will have helped him complete the turn.

To 'set up' his marker, the striker makes it obvious that he is going to give a return pass to the original passer. Most defenders will be relatively happy about the ball being passed away from goal and they are likely to relax. At the last moment, the striker reverses the passing movement of his foot and brings the ball under control. In the same movement he drags the ball sideways and off the line along which the defender is positioned. This move gives him the space and angle to get in his shot.

Professional defenders expect attackers to shoot instantly or at most after one touch. <u>Strikers who occasionally 'stay cool' and risk holding the ball create surprise and, in the right circumstances, outstanding scoring opportunities.</u>

(The more often an attacker tries one particular move, the more his opponents will be ready for it.)

Alternatively the striker may back into the marker and, after threatening to spin off and behind him, moves away from him instead and quickly.

The defender must block any attempt to move behind him and will always be cautious about being drawn away from goal, whatever the temptation.

(A defender can only anticipate what a striker is likely to do based on what he already has done or has tried to do)

A fake first time shot followed by a second and occasionally a third touch shot, or pass, will disconcert a defender. A striker who has two or three options, each of which might lead to a shot, by himself or by someone else, sets enormous problems inside the penalty area.

He has to be treated cautiously. A challenge too early may open up a shooting chance. A challenge too late may lead to a foul and to a penalty.

Drawing defenders into 'no win' situations is one of the hallmarks of great strikers. They must be where the greatest number of scoring chances are likely to occur; if not always, most of the time.

5.116 Surprise and Indirect Moves.

The ability to do the unexpected is an important tactical skill.

Very occasionally, a striker may move into positions comparatively remote from the goal area to attract passes. He does so to test the responses of his marker and of other defenders.

- Are the defenders organized to counter unorthodox moves?
- Does anyone follow him?
- Does anyone pick up other attackers who fill the goal-area position?
- Can he move back into the key striking area without being tracked or marked?

Answers to these questions enable the intelligent striker to explore different tactical options.

The direct approach to scoring must be varied with indirect options in high class soccer. Going through the same motions all the time may work in junior soccer and the striker may score a vast number of goals. And for young and developing players that adds up to valuable practice.

The further he progresses, however, the greater the degrees of craft and cunning he must learn to use.

Learning when, where and how to disappear and to reappear are valuable skills. They can be learned through trial and success. . . in other words through practice.

Alfredo Di Stefano of Argentina was, arguably, the greatest play maker and goal scorer of all time. He could play anywhere, as the situation demanded. Understandably, he was the focus of intense defensive attention. Di Stefano developed an Houdini-like vanishing skill. He could vanish from play in an instant, leaving worried and very nervous defenders searching for him. When he reappeared, always close to goal, it was to deliver the killing shot.

5.12 In and close to the penalty area, without the ball, the striker uses tactical 'know how' to create scoring opportunities for other players or to create alternative, better passing options for players 'on' the ball. He moves to inconvenience, to the greatest possible extent, all marking or covering defenders.

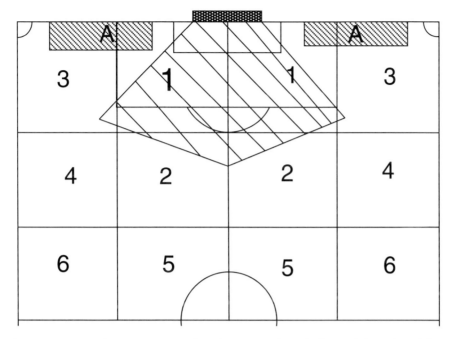

Diagram 7. *Attacking areas in order of priority. The side boxes 'A' are key delivery areas.*

5.121 Decoy Moves.

Persuading defenders to leave areas which, if penetrated, offer optimum scoring chances, requires a deep appreciation of what defenders are or are not likely to do in any set of circumstances. Added to that must be a constant awareness of the movements and the positioning of other players, attackers and defenders, around him.

Strikers must understand what defenders' action priorities are in these areas. With that understanding will come an appreciation of probability: the probability that certain actions by strikers will cause certain reactions from defenders. Understanding that is knowing how to manipulate defenders.

In diagram 7, the lower the number in a square the more important it is from a scoring point of view. The numbers are paired because each position is duplicated in the other half of the pitch.

In diagram 8 the striker, white 10, fixes his marker as white 4 attacks the same area with the ball. When white 4 is in a position to dribble on and shoot, or perhaps to pass and move for a return pass, the striker pulls away from the marker and to one side.

The marker dare not follow to leave space for the dribble and shot but if he leaves the striker free and chooses to block the dribble, the striker

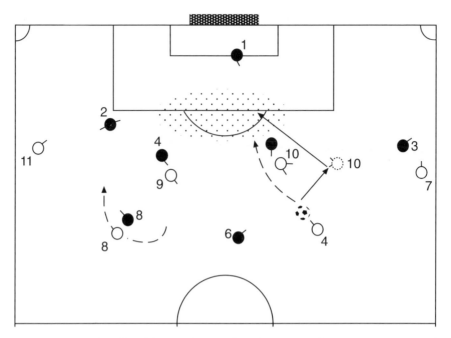

Diagram 8. *A striker 'fixes' his marker to draw him away from important attacking space.*

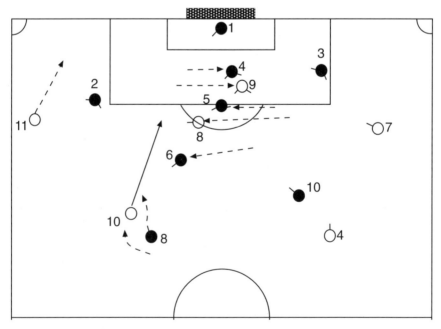

Diagram 9. *Clearing forward space for a crossover move.*

might receive the ball and either shoot or extend the interpassing move with other players. In diagram 8, which shows a back four without a sweeper, imagine how much more difficult life for strikers must be with the shaded area occupied by a free back.

5.122 Clearing Space.
Cleverness in making space through which other attackers can move and set up dangerous situations often goes unnoticed by spectators. It should receive much greater recognition; it is one of the most subtle aspects of a striker's tactical skill.

In diagram 9, the mid-field player, white 10, is about to play a pass into the penalty area. As he sets himself for the pass, the striker, white 9, 'back-pedals' away from the central area and a second striker, white 8, moves past his teammate towards the same area. Both defenders, black 4 and 5, could be confused by this crossover play if the timing is right. Defender black 4 may be reluctant to follow white 9 and the far-side defender, black 5, may not be sure which of the strikers to pick up. A split second of indecision between defenders is long enough to free one or the other of the two strikers. This and similar interchanges between two players depends entirely on timing; the timing of one player's move against another's. The player delivering the pass will usually do so to a player, here white 8, moving onto the ball. A player moving backwards while receiving a pass is not quite so serious a problem for a defender.

5.123 Contra-flow Moves.
In diagram 10, white 8 with the ball, moving across field from right to left, is looking for a shooting opportunity or the chance to pass forward to an attacker in an even better position.

The striker, white 10, is moving through the back defenders in the opposite direction.

The defense must compress against any possibility of a shot and to do so they must move with the flow of the attack i.e. from right to left.

The counter move by white 10 opens up the possibility of a reverse pass through the defense: it creates a reasonable chance for a shot on the turn by white 10. Where the first contra-flow move is followed by a second and even a third, dominating the important spaces in front of goal becomes extremely difficult. A diagonal run across the penalty area will achieve optimum effect when it is restricted to the distance within which effective shots are possible.

A run too far and the striker's shooting angle becomes so wide as to make a shot unlikely to occur or to hit the target.

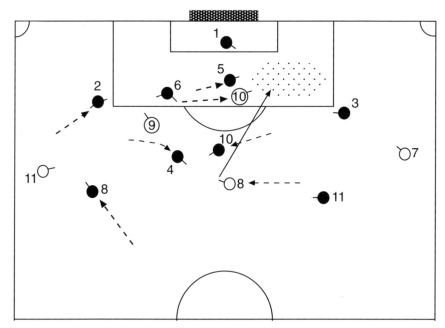

Diagram 10. *Reverse pass moves to unbalance back defenders.*

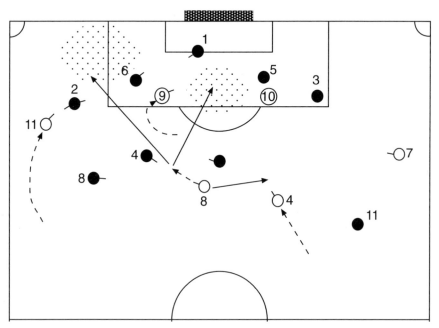

Diagram 11. *Switching the point of attack based on reverse passing.*

5.124 Switching the Point of Attack.

The point of an attack is where one or more attacking players, with the ball, breach or make a concerted effort to breach the opposing defensive curtains.

Following on from the reverse pass move in 5.123, the point of attack may be changed again as in diagram 11. Switching the attacking point is an important tactic against concentrated defenses. And all modern defenses certainly are concentrated.

Switching play causes uncertainty among defenders. In diagram 11, if white 8 can back-heel or stop the ball with the sole of his foot, leaving it for following attacker, white 4, defenders may be caught 'flat-footed' or moving in the wrong direction.

The reverse pass has changed the point of attack in one direction, the back-heel in another.

Continuous player movement across the penalty area following a figure eight pattern, will present frequent and successive targets for dangerous passes. This was the basis of Holland's switch play in their golden years in the seventies including two World Cup finals.

5.125 Unbalancing a Defense.

Where a team uses two strikers in advanced positions both may choose to move towards the ball in order to draw central defenders forward with them. Against twin central backs, this leaves more space behind the central defenders than would otherwise be the case. A quick switch from a central build up to a wide position, diagram 12, may leave a wide defender exposed to a 1 v 1 situation.

This situation again emphasizes the importance of a central defender free to fill space behind tight markers. If the markers are not drawn then either or both of the central attackers will be free to become dangerous play makers. This in itself reinforces my conviction that all players should be all round players.

In diagram 13, the central striker, white 9, has moved out to the wing to support a wide attacking thrust aimed at achieving a good crossing position behind the full back. It is most unlikely that he will be followed all the way. If he is, he will have drawn an important central defender out of position. If not he will have helped to outnumber opponents in an important pre-strike area.

5.21 Operating in the Middle Third of the Pitch.

(with the ball or receiving it).

When defending, all modern players, strikers included, know that their opponents will control the direction and pace of their attacking build-up

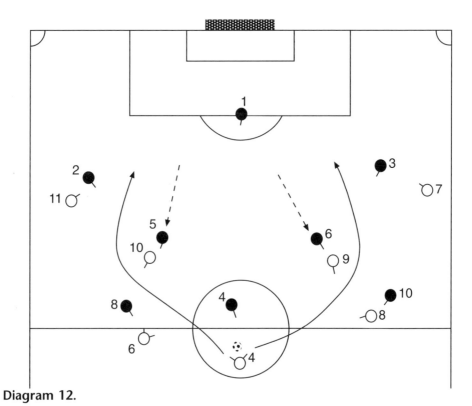

Diagram 12.

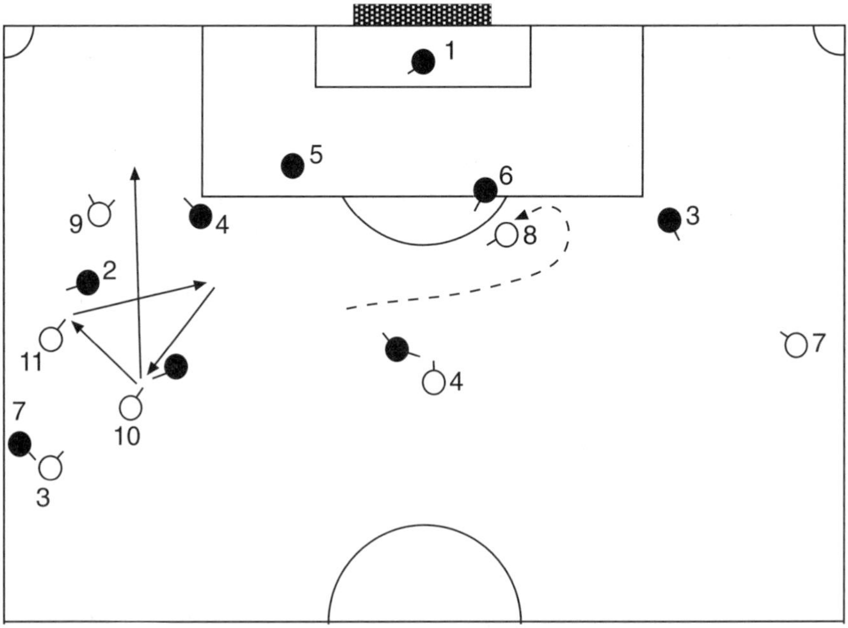

Diagram 13. *Overloading wide defense.*

through their backs: at least in the advanced football countries they will. The striker's function will be to provide a strong, reliable link with those players available to counter attack, to optimize their combined striking capabilities.

Where the striker is likely to receive the ball, his action options are affected by:
   a) the 'strength' of the opposition which he personally faces.
   b) the distance between his receiving position and the opposing goal.
   c) the distance between himself and the nearest supporting player.
   d) the speed with which players move to support him.
   e) the supporting positions which they occupy.
      e.g. behind him, to the sides or in front of him.
   f) the quality of the pass which he receives
   g) his personal technical and athletic skills.

5.211 Relieving Defenders by Holding the Ball.
Having been under severe and sustained pressure, it is unlikely that team-mates will be willing to burst out of defense in numbers to support him. They should of course, and top class coaches will work hard to convince them of the profits to be gained thereby. But expectation has to be tempered by the caution and uncertainty which sustained pressure induces among defenders. The striker will build up their confidence if he can accept the ball, protect it and, if possible, pass to another player who himself should not in any way be embarrassed by the pass.

The striker's teammates want and need a player who can attract the attention of defenders and do enough by himself to give those teammates sufficient time to regain their composure. Composure leads to optimism.

The striker will try all kinds of twists and turns to shake off opponents. However, even if he is successful in turning, he is more than likely to 'fake' moves to press on with the attack. His main aim is likely to be to buy time for supporting players to arrive to establish a more cohesive attacking move.

5.212 Direct Counter Attack - Making Space.
A striker with electric pace will try to draw defenders forward so that any pass out of defense, however far back the delivery point, can be delivered comfortably behind the opposing backs. He tries to shorten the supply lines between the space into which he wants to run and potential passers. Diagram 14.

Alternatively a fast striker might take up position far to one side of the

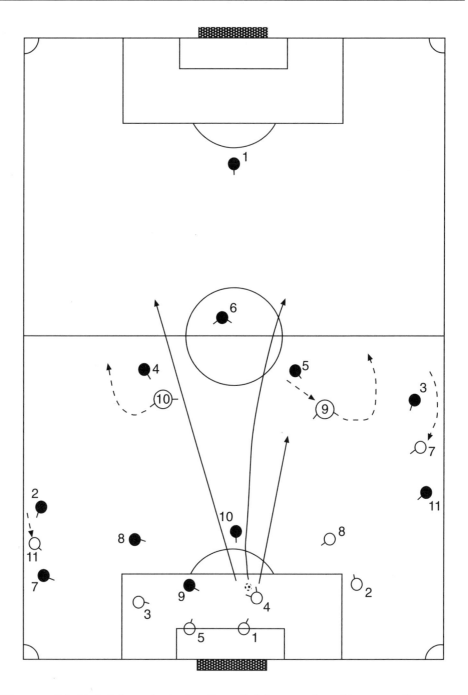

Diagram 14. *First strikers shortening lines of delivery and marking space for delivery.*

pitch and away from a possible direct long pass out from defense. He does so knowing that the ball will be aimed behind defenders on the other side of the pitch or centrally. This pre-arrangement allows him to make a long backward, curved run before bending the run behind defenders into the target area for the pass. Two or even three strikers making these backward curved runs before sprinting forward for the ball pose enormous problems for backs without comparable speed and especially for any trying to use off-side tactics.

Passing to a striker's feet, necessary at times, encourages defenders to risk tackles or interceptions when all the advantages are with the defenders. Defenders will risk fouling opponents where resultant free kicks pose no danger. They may get away with the foul but the striker won't!

5.213 Split Runs.

In diagram 14, the strikers, white 9 and 10, have moved towards their goal and away from each other. Outward curved runs take them back into upfield positions when the ball is played into the space behind them. Against a sweeper and centre back two strikers will often make 'split' runs to reduce the cover which central backs provide for each other.

Where the attack is well to one side of the pitch, the 'far side' striker must attract the attention of the sweeper and 'fix him' as far as possible away from the intended target area, shaded in diagram 15. The strikers may use cross over runs but the ultimate curve towards the space behind the backs is the same.

All tactical moves in attack depend on timing. The curved run into space must be fractionally later than the pass. A run made too early 'gives the game away'; opponents know what the passer is going to do.

5.214 'Long and Short Options.

Occasionally, as we have seen, a striker must 'show' himself for passes to his feet. A teammate, under severe pressure from opponents, may not be able to compose himself for a high quality delivery. As one striker shows himself for a pass to feet, a second striker should attack the space behind his partner. Diagram 16.

The passer then has two options, a pass to feet or a slightly longer pass into space.

If the second option is chosen, the striker who has 'shown' for the pass to feet will spin around his marker quickly to establish support for the advanced striker.

5.215 The 'Third Man'.

If the pass to feet has been chosen, a supporting player. . . preferably two

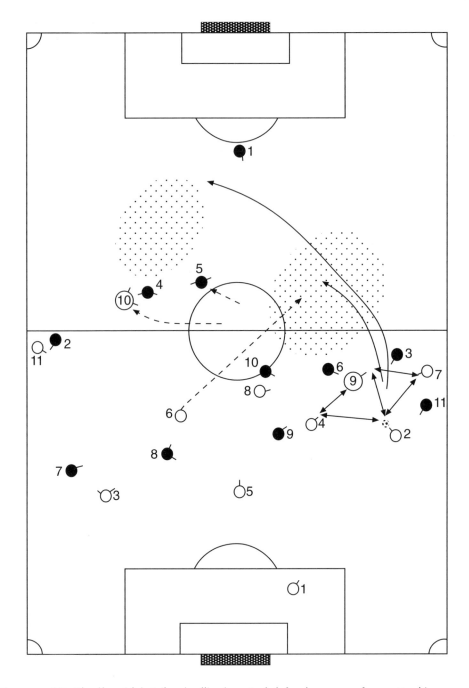

Diagram 15. *The 'far-side' striker 'pulling' central defenders away from attacking target space. (shaded)*

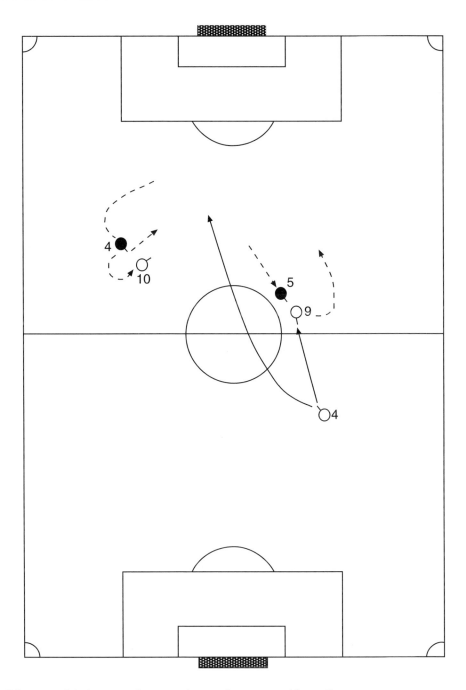

Diagram 16. *Long or short passing options created by strikers.*

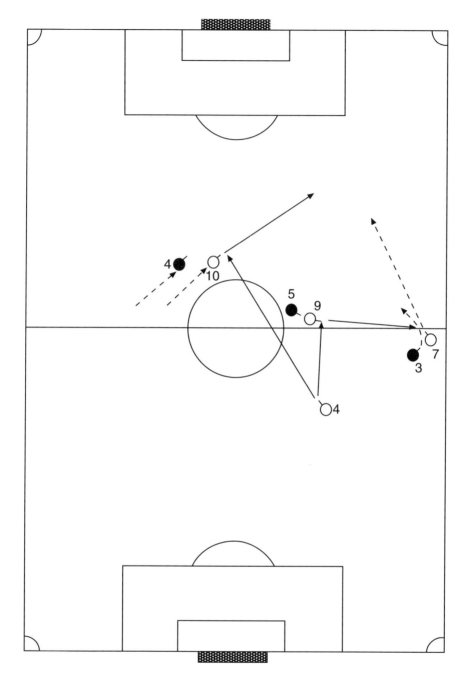

Diagram 17. *Third man moves in any three play interpassing move, the 'third man' must show for a forward pass.*

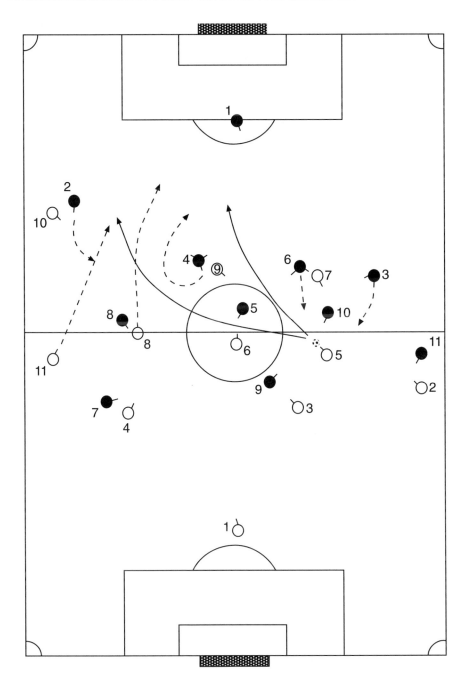

Diagram 18. *Flat back four offside play.*

. . . must make themselves available for a pass 'laid off' by the striker. Diagram 17.

They should be not so close to the striker as to demand too high a degree of 'touch' and accuracy from him and not so far away as to allow opponents time to adjust their marking and covering options.

Whichever of the supporting players receives the 'lay-off' by the striker, the third player must seek a position behind defenders for a forward pass.

Having laid off the pass, the striker will turn off his opponent to seek a similar position in advance of the ball and behind opponents. Diagram 17.

The 'third man' in any such move **MUST** show himself for a forward pass of some kind. If forward runs are not made, penetration isn't possible and the game deteriorates into a negative, go nowhere, passing exercise.

5.216 Off-side Counters.

Defenses, lacking speed in key defensive positions, may base their strategy upon tightly, compressed play in all phases of the game. They may use off-side tactics to assist compression. If play can be compressed into the tightest possible areas for all the players in both teams, each team has equal if reduced chances of success.

You can't get much more negative than that!

Off-side back play, known in England as 'the flat back four', diagram 18, requires defenders to press forward quickly and decisively over a distance of about twenty yards whenever a forward pass looks imminent. As that move takes place, and on a signal, one player. . . the fastest among the backs. . . prepares to drop back. He is the 'fail safe' player. He covers opponents seeking to beat the trap or defenders moving out too slowly to trap opponents in offside positions. He is also insurance against linesmen and referees, notoriously short of visual perception, who allow opponents in doubtful positions to play on.

Off-side decisions by referees and linesmen involve hair-line judgments of where a player happened to be **AT THE MOMENT THE BALL WAS LAST PLAYED**. The difference between being off-side and on-side in top class soccer may be a foot at most. Theoretically it should be inches of course but even referees with the sharpest sight, and there are a few of them about, cannot work to those fine limits!

Defenders are nervous about running forward when a refereeing error could allow an opponent a free run on goal, in the opposite direction and with a twenty yard start into the bargain!

Skillful attackers play upon this nervousness by threatening moves into off-side positions when there is little possibility of the ball being played in their direction. These 'decoy' moves encourage defenders to spring the off-side trap too soon. A striker moves on-side before the pass forward is made which opens up the possibilities for runs made from deeper positions. e.g. white 8 and 11 in diagram 18.

Defeating off-side tactics involves knowing which attackers are making decoy moves to lead opponents into false positions and which are making the real strikes on goal.

Estimating, instantly, the hair's breadth difference between off-side and on-side demands acutely divided attention from attackers. They must practice keeping one eye on the ball player, one eye on the position and movement of the rear-most defender and one eye on the movements of other attackers.

Strikers need three eyes. . . one, preferably, in the backs of their heads!

Where the rearmost defender is central, one or both strikers seek positions on the 'far' side of their markers. Diagram 19. When marked by one defender and covered by another, the sweeper say, the striker is mainly concerned with the position of the sweeper. He will move to a position on the 'far-side' of the sweeper and ignore his marker; he is going to be there anyway.

When strikers move for passes behind defenders curved runs, initially towards play and then into space behind opponents, will pay off.

5.22 Playing Without ('off') the Ball in the Middle Third of the Field.

Effective striker play without the ball in mid-field requires a high degree of persistence with little apparent reward for effort. There are certain basic principles which need to be understood.

(a) Any run towards goal will or is likely to be tracked by a defender.
A move away from goal is less threatening unless there is high probability that it is to receive a pass.

(b) Any run from a wide position centrally probably will attract attention and cause reaction.
A run from a central position away from goal and wide will receive progressively less attention the wider the position.

(c) Angled runs or curved runs, eventually towards goal, provoke the greatest anxiety among central defenders; they don't know what the purpose of the curve or the angle is.

(d) Short, quick movements away from goal started as close to goal as possible and ending perhaps thirty to forty yards from it cause central markers difficulties, particularly those who are poor, or reluctant tight markers.

Runs on the edge of the shooting sector are most likely to attract the greatest attention. Attention is maximized if there is a chance, however remote, of the runner actually receiving the ball.

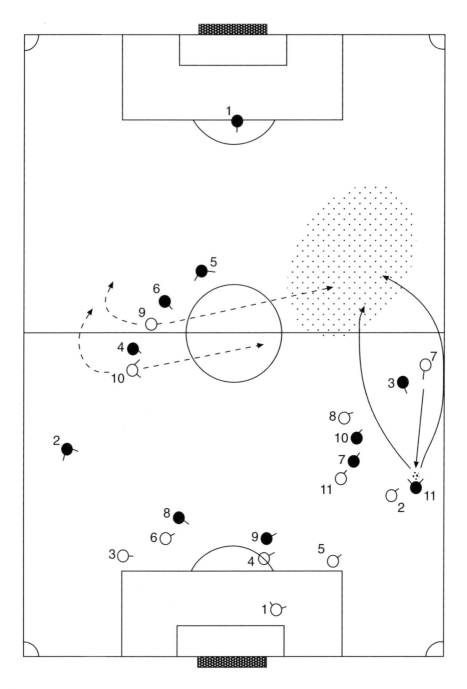

Diagram 19. *Overloading and overbalancing a defense.*

All of that tells us **WHERE** to run but not **HOW** or **WHEN**.

'Off the ball' runs are best made from quick starts, over five yards say, with the player decelerating for the rest of his run.

Quick starts at worst alert defenders, at best frighten them. Defenders, starting late, react by sprinting hard, perhaps too hard, to make up the initial disadvantage. A reactive sprint by a defender may cause that defender to seriously overbalance if his opponent stops or changes direction, particularly the former.

Defenders are always worried by a quick starting attacker who has a smooth change of pace. Controlled acceleration or deceleration allows the striker a degree of composure to accept the ball should it come.

The shock of a quick start by a defender is magnified if it follows a 'fake' move, by a striker, in the opposite direction. A quick twist of the striker's head and shoulders, faking a move in one direction, followed by a fast turn the other way is likely to unbalance an opponent. He cannot be sure what his opponent will do or why he is doing it.

WHEN the move is made is the key to it all.

The first consideration is the availability of another attacker, in a good position, to receive the ball if the decoy move comes off.

Strikers make themselves available for each other, almost intuitively, through many matches played together and lots of practice. . . which are the same thing when you think about it.

Outstanding 'off' the ball players judge, to a split second, when a teammate can begin to deliver the ball. It's not enough just to see him with it, even under perfect control. The player preparing to make a decoy run and therefore the secondary receiver must know where the ball needs to be, on which foot, what the position of his teammate's body should be, the speed at which he is moving and so on if he is to predict the actual delivery of the pass. When all the signs are right or as near right as can be expected, the player off the ball will start his run. Defenders aren't fooled by any sort of move. Their 'trade' is to read opponents' capabilities just as accurately as anyone else.

Laying down false clues depends upon out of the ordinary acting ability. And great actors act naturally.

5.221 Making Space for Mid-field Support Players.

Many negative, professional teams, compress play (players) into the smallest areas possible making a controlled, clever build up of attacking moves very difficult. Mid-field, the area within which attacking play normally is initiated, has been subjected to very high pressure. Increasing numbers of players deployed there have almost destroyed mid-field space and players' time to exercise skill.

It is not unusual, during a professional game, for twenty players to occupy a playing space at most twenty five to thirty yards deep and say seventy yards or so in width. That area filled by all of the outfield players moves from one end towards the other and back according to the ebb and flow of play. To all intents and purposes the whole of both teams are midfield players.

Space and time for a player trying to employ individual skills are at a premium. Players have no time to consider action options after the ball has arrived. Either they know what to do before the ball arrives or both ball and opponents arrive at the same time. . . painfully often.

Strikers can best affect the space available in mid-field by keeping out of it!

When the rest of their team is defending close to goal, strikers may seek positions as far upfield as their opponents and the off- side law will allow. They will take markers with them and, usually, a covering player as well. Movements away from probable lines of attack will draw markers in the same direction: at least until the move becomes negative. A move becomes negative when it ceases to threaten key defensive areas. These decoy moves should be curved or sharply angular. On a curved run the striker will drift rather than sprint: on an angled run his movements will be sharper especially when he changes the angle. The first is used to persuade defenders to follow: the second frightens them into following.

Early in a match, a striker will test markers' responses to his movements, particularly to various kinds of runs.

5.222 Overloading Defenses.

In diagram 19(a), both strikers have moved to positions furthest from the area through which a 'break-out' seems likely. Markers have followed and the sweeper, black 5, has moved nearer to goal into a covering position. In the event of a break out the faster of the two strikers will normally take on the longer run although it must be remembered that a flying start is the best way of defeating opponents who are obliged to start second. If both strikers, white 9 and 10, go for the space on the other side of the pitch, they are almost certain to pull three opponents with them. These moves will ruin the defensive shape of the black team leaving vast spaces for quick thinking white counter attackers moving from defensive posi-tions.

In diagram 20, a wide attacker, white 11, has withdrawn into mid-field while his team develops an attack on the other side of the pitch. If black 2 follows the defense will be unbalanced, leaving space into which other opposing attackers can move. If black 2 doesn't follow white 11, who will stop attacking play developing through him?

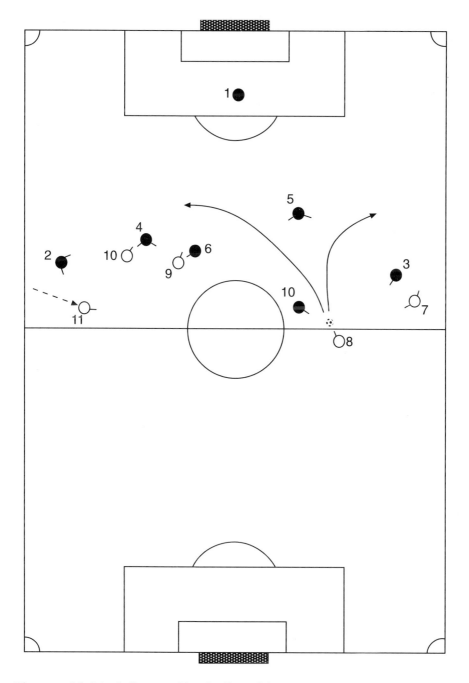

Diagram 19 (a): *Strikers working for 'far-side' positions against markers to produce covering problems for sweeper, black 5.*

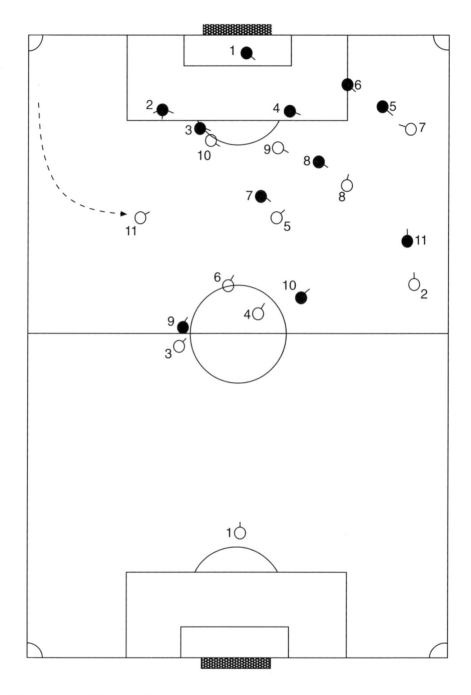

Diagram 20. *Wide attacker assuming unorthodox positions trying to destabilize defensive organization.*

5.223 Stretching the Backs.

In diagram 21, the white strikers, 9 and 10, have pulled wide of the sweeper, remaining fractionally on-side, 'persuading' their opponents to move away from the break-out area. Wide attackers have moved as wide as possible and towards their own wide backs. The 'half-way' positions, between the sweeper and each wide back, make it difficult for the sweeper to cover. Either he calls for off-side tactics or he drops further back to 'read' play and move across to challenge or intercept.

The strikers' positions also threaten space behind or inside the wide backs who may retreat into more central positions to cover those threats. The threats are more imaginary than real. Without a sweeper, centre backs must mark strikers 'one to one' and, hopefully, offer some sort of cover to each other. Strikers will be more than pleased to accept one to one situations. A stubborn refusal to adopt the sweeper system in primary defense and develop mid-field attacking possibilities out of its stabilizing influence has been the biggest single obstacle to England resuming any sort of position as a major soccer power during the last twenty five years. Why? Because sweeper play was outside the playing experience of most British managers and coaches, they didn't know. . . or want to know. . . how to coach it.

5.224 Rotation (Whirling) Play.

The idea of continuous player movements into and out of key attacking areas was first proposed by a great European soccer 'brain', Austria's Willi Meisl, more than fifty years ago. Dr. Meisl realized that players occupying fixed positions in attack, particularly near to goal, exert a similar effect on other players. Play loses fluidity and becomes 'trench warfare', one side hammering away at the other brainlessly.

Fluid play, for Willi Meisl, needed all or most players to be capable of functioning in different positions effectively and frequently.

Movement (rotation) can be in any direction and only stops when opponents become reluctant to follow or actually cease to follow, thereby leaving the rotating players relatively unmarked in important striking positions.

In diagram 22, the two white strikers, 9 and 10, have moved wide as the break-out from defense begins, through white 6 for example. If the counter-attack develops centrally, they 'bend' their runs back towards their own mid-field. While markers follow they continue this move and mid-field players move forward to replace them as advanced strikers. When markers refuse to follow and hold central defensive positions, strikers 'bend' their movements into positions behind forward moving mid-field players. When marked one to one, strikers try to draw markers

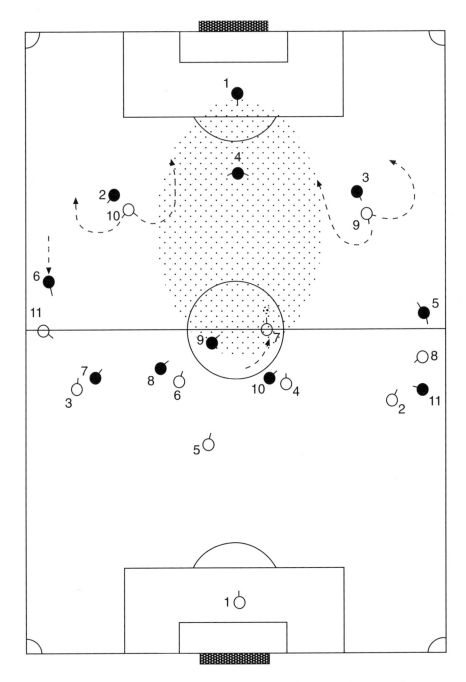

Diagram 21. *Stretching the backs by maximizing the space between them.*

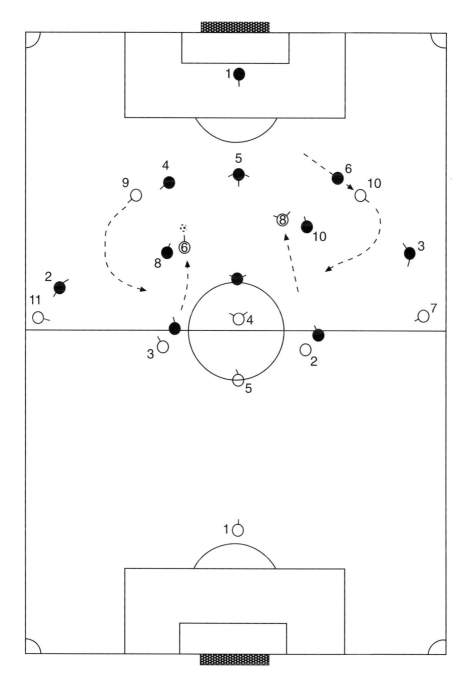

Diagram 22. *Circulating positional interchanges.*

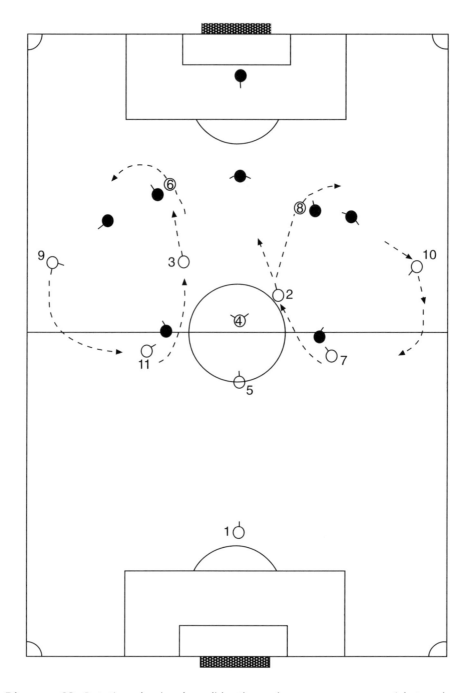

Diagram 23. *Rotation play 'anchored' by three players: a sweeper, a picket and a goalkeeper.*

into positions half-way towards other defenders' areas of responsibility. Defenders dislike decisions forced on them by 'off the ball' moves, the purposes of which are unclear.

Rotation play is highly effective near to the penalty area. It can also pose difficult problems for defenders in mid-field especially when the defenders' own mid-field players have been drawn forward and have lost the ball.

Backs are comfortable when they have a defensive curtain of players in front of them; without it they may find themselves drawn into positions where they must react to strikers' moves and where, if their zonal relationships are breached, opposing attackers may move, unmarked, onto the ball for strikes at goal. In diagram 23, all the outfield players can tolerate except the sweeper white 5 and the picket player white 4. They are the 'fail safe' elements and there is no reason why they shouldn't rotate into attacking positions if they are confident that their defensive anchor roles will be filled temporarily and competently.

The only fear involved in fluid team play is that players moving into adventurous positions might be let down. The coach has to sort that problem out.

5.225 Stitching up the Backs.

Any move from wide on one side of the field to wide on the other, in and out of the backs, sets problems. Defenders are never sure if, when or where the runner will bend his stitching (in and out) run towards goal, diagram 24, and they cannot be sure about catching him offside. In diagram 24, the two strikers have moved touch-line wide. When a break-out from defense is 'on', one or both move across field, sometimes running in front of defenders and sometimes threatening the space behind them. Defenders must cover the runs because either player could change his flat run into a direct run on goal should a long pass be possible. This may cause the backs, especially the slower ones, to drop back in anticipation of 'through' pass possibilities.

The cross field moves must be tracked by defenders who are likely to compress as each runner moves from one defensive zone into another.

Stitching runs' were used to great effect by Gadocha, Poland's wing striker in their 1974 World Cup semi-final team. Gadocha's cross-field runs were quick, close to the backs and likely to be 'bent' towards goal for a through pass at any time. Off-side verdicts were always hair-line and far too close for defensive comfort since the player watched for off-side attempts carefully. Running from a wide position furthest from a potential passer he was easily able to watch both the ball and at least one defender thereby making it very difficult for defenders to trap him offside. These runs might be even more effective as a result of the modification of the off-side law in recent years.

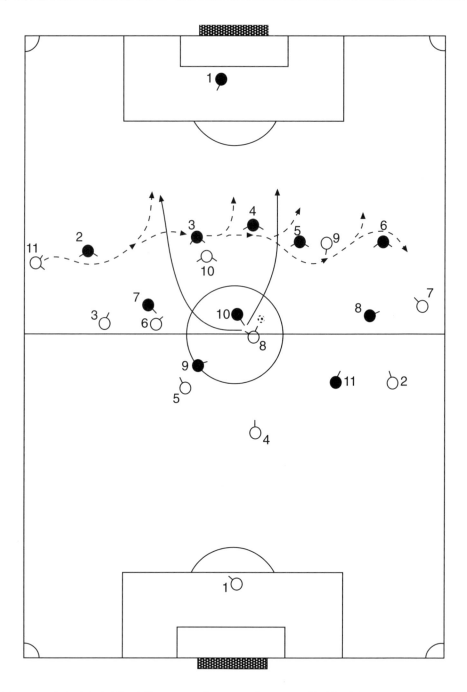

Diagram 24. *A 'stitching' (in and out) run to threaten off-side risks.*

Chapter 6
Important Technical Skills and Principles

rom the definition of the striker's role, his responsibilities and the identification of the personal tactical skills he needs to fulfill that role, we can identify the special techniques upon which tactical effectiveness will depend. All soccer players, irrespective of positions, must master the fundamental techniques involved in controlling the ball, dribbling, passing, shooting, heading, tackling, intercepting and so on to the highest degrees of accuracy, sensitivity and deception. The following section deals with the action principles which govern the important techniques for all strikers; those which give strikers much needed advantages in their battles against defensive strangulation.

6.1 Shooting Skills.

A striker whose scoring rate averages less than a goal every other game needs a coach's help and a lot of practice. He may make goals for others but top strikers do that and score themselves. . . very frequently; opponents, intimidated by exceptional scoring abilities, pay less attention than they should to other attackers.

Effective shooting is based upon the following priorities.

a) **Being willing to shoot and willing to risk missing!**
   Whenever a striker shoots he should score. . . couch critics say so! The pressures to score may be so great that some players opt out.
   Consistent scorers have the determination and the skill to get in their shots together with the courage to ignore failure.

   Stanley Matthews, one of the greatest wing players of all time, rarely attempted to score. From simple scoring positions, Matthews would pass to other attackers to shoot; sometimes they missed.

   Matthews, a perfectionist in practice, training and in every other aspect of play, wouldn't risk failing to score; for him it probably represented the ultimate imperfection.

   There are different kinds of courage in soccer. The courage to make a decision and to accept responsibility for the consequence is important. Taking a penalty in the last minutes of The World Cup Final, with the score at 0-0, in front of 100,000 stadium spectators and

2,000,000,000 television experts, all of whom would certainly score, requires nerves of. . . well steel might not be tough enough.

b) Shooting and Hitting the Target.

Shooting and failing to hit the target is not easily forgivable, even when shooting under the most intense pressure.

Forget bad luck; soccer is a game of skill, not of chance. However weak the shot, if it is on target the wind, a bump on the pitch or even a goalkeeper error may cause the ball to enter the net: off target and there is no chance.

c) Expecting the Ball and a Shooting Chance.

The great strikers expect the ball to arrive in a shooting position all the time. They 'know' that the ball will come, even when it doesn't!

High expectation is fundamental to anticipation. Top marksmen are always mentally prepared for a shooting opportunity. This state of readiness is the starting point for preparing their feet, their legs and the rest of their bodies to assume effective shooting 'shapes'. If the feet are positioned wrongly certain forms of leg swing are not possible. If the upper body is allowed to twist freely during shooting, control of direction becomes impossible.

d) Shooting Sight Lines.

Goalscorers rarely have time to judge the flight of the ball, to prepare for the actual shot while assessing the position of the goalkeeper and the probability of his reaction to this shot or that. Goal scorers 'know' where the 'keeper is and what he is doing all the time. Their minds record that information much like a video recorder and they have instant play-back built in. In common with other cunning players they are never caught actually assessing a goalkeeper's options. Their eyes never give them away.

Having calculated the target angle and distance, goal scorers 'see' the line from their foot through the required impact point which, when extended, passes through the precise target aimed for.

e) Ignoring Distractions.

Having programmed their mental computers, 'sharp-shooters' give all their attention to striking the ball exactly where and how a shot on target demands. The imminent challenge of one or more defenders, the distracting actions of the goalkeeper, interference from his own players, all are shut out as the striker concentrates exclusively on striking the ball as perfectly as putting the ball in the back of the net requires.

Shooting accurately involves no more than passing the ball between two posts, under a cross-bar and beyond an opponent who can use any part of his body to stop the ball.

Allowing for the goalkeeper's advantages, striking a ball to pass through a target eight yards wide and eight feet high should present few problems.

Those then are the priorities for a super marksman. They indicate where the balance of his practice should be located.

6.11 Principles.
Before setting down the 'how', 'where' and 'when' of different shooting skills it is necessary that players, and coaches, understand certain simple principles which will affect the result of a shot on goal whatever the skill used.

(a) Direction and Power.
The precise and relatively small point of impact between foot and ball through which a line of force is developed towards the target governs direction.

Any action which alters the angle of leg swing and thereby the line of force from the foot through the ball to the target will affect accuracy.

b) Force applied to the ball through any point BELOW its horizontal mid-line will cause the ball to rise and usually to spin backwards. The lower the point of impact, the greater the back spin, the greater the 'lift' and the less the distance carried.

c) Force applied through any point ABOVE the same mid-line directs the ball downwards and results in top spin and often dip through the air.

d) Force applied to one side or the other of a vertical mid-line, causes the ball to spin and swerve in the opposite direction.

e) Finally, force applied below the horizontal mid-line and to the left of the vertical mid-line will cause the ball to spin, to lift and to swerve from left to right and vice versa.

As points of impact are moved off the imaginary mid-line which points horizontally towards the target, the greater the resultant effects of lift, spin and swerve until, of course, the line of force is off the ball entirely which results in a mis-kick or slice.

Very young players should be encouraged to experiment with swerve and spin especially with and against wind. They should develop an understanding of the effects of kicking through different impact points. Spin and swerve enable a player to deliver highly deceptive passes and shots.

f) Power for the kick (shot) is a product of the speed at which the player's foot is traveling when it hits the ball and the length of time the foot stays in contact with the ball. Obviously there are a number of considerations which affect the speed of a player's kicking foot; they are beyond the scope of this particular book.

A 'natural' kicking action involves swinging the kicking leg across the body; this allows the kicker to remain well balanced throughout the kick. Leg swing causes the rest of the body, except the arms, from the hips upwards, to tend to follow the swing. The arms swing in the opposite direction to the kicking foot enabling the player to remain balanced.

The more powerful the leg swing, the greater the twist tendency.

The more powerful the twist, the greater the transfer of its effect through the rest of the body.

Body twist may become so exaggerated that it controls the leg swing; the opposite should be the case. Limitation of the twist effect is best contrived by increasing the 'round the corner' approach to the kicking position and thereby to the target line. Alternatively, holding the front shoulder firmly towards the target will prevent it from swinging wide of the target thereby allowing the kicking foot to follow the same line.

The direction along which the standing foot points as kicking contact is made will also affect body turn. Where the standing foot is pointing forward, there are almost unlimited opportunities for a chest position fully open to the target. That means the leg swing can finish with the toe pointing in almost any direction. . . and so can the ball. Where the standing foot points across the line of the kick, the foot effectively locks the hips and prevents excessive body turn or twist.

The control exerted by different body positions and by different foot positions on body turn and thereby on shooting direction must be understood and practiced by all players who hope to become exceptional goal scorers.

6.12 Shooting on The Run.

When running forward to shoot, most strikers prefer to shoot from an angle, a position to one side of the goal, rather than from a central position. This allows for a natural leg swing slightly across the body. If the contact is fractionally inaccurate or if the leg swing is minimally too far across the body, the resultant kick tends to be 'pulled', i.e. a right foot shot tends to move further than required from right to left and vice versa.

Moving onto a wider angle before shooting, enables the striker to 'allow' for this pull. Of course it also gives the goalkeeper some indication of the striker's intentions and allows him to narrow the shooting angle from his point of view and thereby reduce the size of the target behind him.

Wide angle shooting positions mean that a striker must master shooting with swerve to enable him to shoot past the 'keeper and bend the ball back into goal.

Power shooting, for the sake of it, fools no one and is a matter of hope rather than expectation.

A widened shooting angle gives a striker a sizable target area inside the far post and a nearer but smaller target option at the near post. A shot inside the far post often is the better choice. If the goalkeeper deflects the shot or the shot is 'pulled' wide of the far post, another attacker may get to it and score. Attackers must be alert for second chances; world class strikers score many of their goals from these situations.

Sustained concentration is necessary for anticipating such possibilities, luck doesn't enter into it.

Having set up a shooting angle: having selected his target: having estimated the distance from the goalkeeper at which he intends to shoot, the final decision determines how much power will be required to shoot beyond the goalkeeper's reach before he can move to save.

Decisions made while the goalkeeper is moving forward are likely to favor the chance of a goal being scored. A forward moving goalkeeper is more easily beaten than one set and in position to make a save.

Reference was made earlier to the 'near' post target option. Occasionally a striker may fake this option because the shooting position which is needed will, with a minor change of contact on the ball, serve for the far post shot as well. The reverse is not the case. To change from the shooting position which he needs for a far post shot to one inside the near post may require the striker to hit the ball with the outside of his shooting foot if he is to make a last second change but not so much as to produce serious swerve effect.

Striking a ball accurately off-centre, as this shot requires and at the very last split second, is a very difficult skill: not impossible but definitely difficult.

A striker running in on goal has other shooting options of course. He can fake a shot but dribble the ball round the goalkeeper to score.

He can also fake a shot off the obvious foot and change the ball to his other foot at the last moment. Change of foot alters the shooting angle entirely and gives the goalkeeper almost no time in which to re-adjust his position, however extra time allows him to gain a position closer to the striker.

If a foot change is the striker's intention, it will be to his advantage to make his first shooting angle in favor of a shot from his weaker foot. . . unless the goalkeeper knows which his weaker foot is!

When he switches the ball to his other, stronger foot, he has a much wider shooting angle, making more of the target available.

At the highest level, goalkeeper's need only one look at an opponent's play and his strengths and weaknesses are filed away for all time.

Occasionally, a striker has a long run at goal, having received the ball just over the halfway line perhaps. The goalkeeper will want to narrow the striker's shooting angle completely and to do so he will come out further than he might wish to do in different circumstances. He has nothing to lose.

The striker now has the options discussed previously plus the additional option of shooting (chipping) over the goalkeeper's head. His decision will be based on the space he needs behind the goalkeeper into which his lobbed or chipped shot will travel and the distance in front of the goalkeeper which will enable him to clear the goalkeeper's fully stretched jump. All strikers leave themselves some margin of error. The better they are the smaller the margin they need.

'Chipping' a ball which is running away from a player himself running at speed is a top skill but the greater the space (time) available the more of an acceptable shooting option it becomes.

6.13 Chipping.

To achieve optimum height to clear a goalkeeper using a fully stretched jump, (a total height of roughly ten feet), and with little space in which to land the ball, a striker needs time to set himself for the chip. Judging approach distance, height and 'carry' is a complex judgment. The complexity of the problem is intensified because both goalkeeper and the striker are likely to be moving towards each other, thereby changing the distance and consequently the height relationships all the time.

The ball must be struck beneath its contact point with the ground taking out the top surface of the ground. This should produce optimum lift and back spin. The more the foot strikes through a part of the ball rather than under it, the less the back spin and the lower the lift.

A strike too far under the ball may produce too much height and excessive back spin which may prevent the ball 'carrying' into goal; too little back spin and the lack of lift may allow the 'keeper to save the shot.

The kicking leg is fully bent during the back swing and the first phase of down swing.

In the phase leading to contact under the ball the foot must travel very quickly to maximize back spin and to compensate for the ball moving away from the kicker. Forward rotation on the ball is changed into very fast backward rotation (spin). Increasing the speed of the striking foot requires the bent knee to be straightened very quickly to accelerate the foot to the required contact point underneath the ball. Almost all of the leg swing to the strike comes from the knee: very little from the hip. The 'feel' of an effective 'chip' is that of brushing underneath the ball with the top part of the toes and lower instep. A player should 'feel' that the kick has been achieved with little resistance from the ball. It has!
The leg swing and the strike beneath the ball are best achieved from a ball positioned well off to one side of the striker.

6.14 Half-volley Shooting.

In and near to the penalty, strikers are rarely allowed the luxury of time . . . at least not by determined opponents. Shooting chances occur when the striker has almost no time to set himself into this position or that shape. Even with one controlling touch, the shot will have to be taken as the ball hits the ground, on the half volley. More likely, the shot will have to be completed first touch, on the volley or half volley and in all likelihood while the striker is turning.

A player needs to 'see' his shooting line instantly. This enables him to prepare his body' shape' and adjust his standing foot while retaining his line of sight to his target.

For a half volley, the standing foot is placed close to and inside the point at which the player imagines the ball will strike the ground. The swing of the striking leg begins with a bent knee which accelerates and straightens smoothly and powerfully in time with the ball dropping to the ground. The player concentrates on timing the arrival of his foot, at the required speed, to strike through the imagined contact point on the ball exactly as the ball hits it. A fraction late and he will lift his shot high; a fraction early and he will 'top' his shot and lose power and direction. The secret of control is the follow through of the player's shooting foot which must be held towards the target until the ball has left it, not when it is about to! Both contact and follow through are along the line which the player 'sees' ending on target.

The player's weight should continue moving towards the imagined contact point between ball and ground as his leg snaps straight and his foot strikes the ball. The standing foot may have to turn slightly to adjust for slight miscalculations of ball flight or for the appearance of unforeseen obstacles to an effective shot.

The key to effective half-volleying is the timing of the foot swing to coincide with the drop of the ball.

Half volleys are powerful shooting options because the ball has little if any inertia and offers very low resistance to the kick. The ball being only fractionally off the ground when struck, the kicking leg can be at full stretch and the kicking foot accelerating at optimum speed at impact, hence the effortless power of a well timed half volley.

6.15 Volley Shooting.

Shooting on the volley, that is to say when the ball is off the ground, presents similar problems for sighting the target and lining up the shot. The striker imagines the line through the ball from his swinging foot to the required target area. Having 'seen' the line the need is to alter the body position to enable the shooting foot to pass through the ball and towards the target area while directing the ball's line of flight precisely.

The higher the ball when struck, the more the striker will have to lean . . . or fall. . . away from the ball. Falling away from the ball enables him to raise the hip of his shooting leg and consequently the leg, knee and foot into positions from which the required line of strike and follow through can be achieved. When a volley is attempted above hip height, the player may have to become fully airborne to develop the leg swing to strike and follow through along the right 'line'.

Controlled 'body turn' is an important aspect of volley shooting. Without body turn and the additional power produced, the striker has only leg and foot speed with which to generate power; the position from which the shot has to be executed makes power from this source limited.

Having 'read' the direction and the probable height at which the ball will arrive, and having mentally 'lined up' his shot the player almost turns his back to the target. As the ball approaches, first his head, then his arms and shoulders, then his hips and finally his shooting leg and foot, are turned powerfully into contact and follow through.

His body is coiled away from goal like a spring before being released into the shot.

The secret for high volley shooting is this coiled, back-to-the -target 'shape' which the player assumes before the ball arrives.

6.16 Overhead Shooting.

Occasionally a striker's only opportunity for a shot is when the ball is at head height or even higher. He may also find himself nearer to goal than the ball's line of flight. Here he turns his back fully towards goal. The non kicking leg is kicked high in the air immediately followed by his kicking (shooting) leg to make contact with the ball. This double leg action produces what is called a scissor kick; the player is in the air and falling backwards as he hits the ball. In falling backwards, his leg and foot swing is likely to be on a downward path as it contacts the ball helping to keep the shot on target. The striker must be fully airborne to enable him to strike through the ball downwards. Power generated in the shooting leg is developed by using the preliminary swing of the first part of the scissor movement.

Without this initial, opposing movement it would be impossible to generate effective power through his shooting leg.

When kicking overhead, a striker must be certain that nearby players are not in danger of being 'volleyed'. Having committed himself to an overhead shot, the action cannot be stopped or redirected; in a crowded goalmouth it may be dangerous.

Getting airborne is easy, landing is difficult and often painful. A player may land on his upper back and lower neck painfully. He must use his hands and forearms to try to strike the ground before his body lands; they will absorb most of the shock of landing.

Painful or not, scoring a great goal will be worth it!

Any or all of the basic kicking and passing techniques may be used by a striker to score goals. In the case of shooting for goal, the end result is more important than the methods used or the elegance of execution. If a striker scores with the back of his neck or with his knee, the goal counts just as much as if he had scored with a clinically accurate and effortlessly executed shot. Gerd Muller, Germany's 1974 goal fountain, frequently scored with the unlikely parts of his anatomy: some unmentionable.

Forgive the repetition but goal scoring does depend upon a player's determination to be first to the ball.

Getting some part of his body to the ball in front of a defender will give a striker every chance of scoring in any company. A 'waiter', a player who waits to see what will happen or waits for the time and space for a shot will be lucky to score at all.

6.2 Attacking Headers.

The techniques used when heading for goal are exactly those used when heading in any phase of the game. The flat frontal part of the forehead is always used for accurate, power headers. The sides of the forehead may be used for flick headers and the front top of the head used for back headers. The greater the use of the front of the forehead, the greater the control over direction and the greater the power generated.

Heading power will be increased when a striker can:
   (a) run and jump into the heading position.
   (b) arch his back and his neck as he jumps.
   (c) jack-knife his body forward as he nears the point of contact with the ball.
   (d) finally use his neck muscles to punch his head through the ball towards the target.

The secret of successful jump headers is in selecting the position from which to start the run for take-off. Too many player want to be immediately beneath the ball when they jump.

This means that one or more defenders will take off from roughly the same position. Even worse, it means that the striker must take off vertically with almost no run. Anyone able to do so successfully should give up soccer, he would be a certainty for Olympic high jump gold.

Strikers must give themselves the longest possible approach run.

In diagram 25, the striker, white 9, has moved well away from and beyond the key striking areas close to goal. Fractionally before the ball is crossed, the striker begins his run into target area: T1 and T2 in the diagram.

A defender has probably tracked the striker into the wide position. Even so, all advantages will be with the striker. He knows the intended dropping areas; he starts the race and he is running in to meet the ball. The defender follows the same path but has to try to head it in the opposite direction almost. The player who starts the race in soccer always wins. . . or should.

Well organized teams pre-arrange the areas towards which crosses will be aimed from certain positions. For example, in diagram 25, the likely target areas may be T1 and T2. If enough attackers are within traveling distance of the penalty area at the anticipated time of the cross, all three target areas might be attacked at the same time.

The crossing player doesn't pick out a target player, his responsibility is to deliver good crosses into one of the three areas. The timing of the arrival of the attackers is their responsibility. When crossing players try to

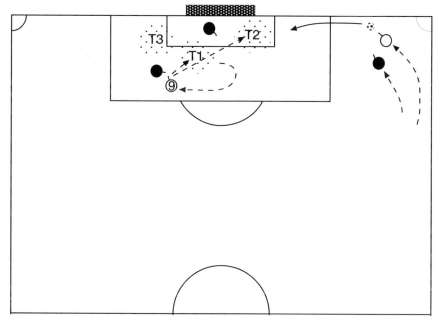

Diagram 25. *Attacking target areas for crosses.*

judge the approach run of attackers while assessing the threats posed by markers or covering players, the whole business becomes a subject for too many 'ifs'. When all players share a clear and simple plan of action, success is more likely.

All kinds of fake moves may be used by strikers to enable them to get into the best heading positions. These moves are strictly between the attackers and their opponents; all that the wide player needs to bother about is delivering accurate crosses into pre-determined areas.

Which strikers get there; how they get there; where from and when they start their runs to get there is nothing to do with the ball crossers.

Take-off techniques are exactly the same as for high jumping in any sport.

A long stride pre-take-off leads into thrust from the take-off foot and a powerful upward swing of the free leg. Upward arm swings assist the lift.

A very firm inside arm, the arm nearest to the opponent, can provide useful protection against the challenge of opponents and some protection against a possible clash of heads.

'To get ahead, get in front' is the motto to be used by all strikers, however skillful they may be at jumping very high to head for goal. Too often strikers with a better jump than opponents or a significant height advantage choose to jump behind and over defenders; they are wrong.

The striker may fake a move behind his opponent before attacking the space in front of him. When the target area for the cross is in the near post area, T2 in diagram 25, the striker may use a flick header towards goal or a back header to another striker. Now, the timing of his run for the target area is more important than the quality of his take off since he will not be jumping to achieve great height. He **WILL** be jumping to be first to the ball. It may even be necessary to use a jump and dive to be first there. Flick headers or back headers to other attackers pose great difficulties for defenders, especially for goalkeepers. They have very little time in which to make considered judgments and are forced to react to the flicks with little if any time in which to prepare to challenge for the ball or to make a save.

Even headers which have to be attempted in strange circumstances, when diving or falling backwards for example, must use the flat frontal part of the forehead. . . if at all possible. The use of the neck muscles, in the final analysis, is the only way to generate power with control. The head is first twisted away from the ball and then 'thrown' at it. The flat front of the forehead is turned back to strike through the ball at the same time.

Back headers are played off the part of the head where the hair-line meets the forehead. . . in young players that is!

6.3 Controlling and Turning with the Ball.
All the basic controlling techniques must be acquired. Strikers are subjected to very tight marking and to fierce challenges for possession of the ball. Trapping and controlling techniques must stand up to the most severe pressure from opponents.

6.31 Open Turn.
Strikers must learn to control the ball and to turn in one movement and often with only one touch of the ball. The striker moves down the line of the oncoming ball. Depending on the ball speed, when the ball is two or three yards away he turns half sideways and as the ball reaches his foot he completes the turn, allowing the controlling foot, the rear foot, to 'give' with the ball. The striker's 'side on' position enables him to split his vision of both ball and marker.

Markers enjoy 'going in' for the ball when a striker's attention is focused entirely on controlling it; they can't see what is coming!

The turning technique can be varied if, instead of allowing his controlling foot to 'give' with the ball, he pulls that foot sharply across the back of the ball, wrapping his foot around it as he does so. This enables the player to pull the ball away from a possible tackling attempt while completing his turn in the same movement.

6.32 Letting The Ball Run.
Very popular with Scottish players I am told but long before my time.

The best strikers become adept at 'faking' movements to create uncertainty in the minds of defenders. Letting the ball run is a useful example. As a pass is played up to the striker he moves towards it and shows his marker enough of the ball to tempt him to try to intercept it. As the defender does so, the striker moves his body firmly across his opponent's line of attack and allows the ball to run past on his other side. The firmer the defender's commitment to interception, the greater the blocking effect of the striker's body which helps him to turn while throwing the defender off balance.

Letting the ball run requires strikers to be very good judges of a ball's pace and to be both quick, late and strong when turning 'off' and blocking his opponent. If a striker shows his intention to let the ball run he will be 'grassed': another Scottish expression.

6.33 Turning Off A Marker.
A striker can use tight marking to his advantage when receiving passes 'to feet'. If he leans back into his marker, the striker effectively fixes him. Strictly speaking the striker can only lean back into his marker when the ball is within playing distance. If the striker takes up such a position before the ball is within playing distance he is guilty of obstruction; not a lot of referees seem to know this. In either case, the defender cannot tackle or intercept, indeed he may struggle to even see the ball. The striker can sometimes affect an opponent's balance so much that he can turn off and around him while holding the ball. Dalglish, a famous Scottish international striker and now a successful coach, used this technique to great advantage especially near to the penalty area where, having half turned around his marker, a shooting chance often presented itself. When turning, the striker will find a very strong inside arm useful in preventing the marker from regaining a challenging position. The difference between a fair (legal) technique and an illegal practice is on a very fine line.

Mr. Dalgish, being small and innocent looking, almost always got the benefit of referees' doubts.

All attacking skills must contain an element of surprise.

A striker who can produce unexpected skills and techniques frightens opponents: when those skills are used with variation in pace and acceleration even more so. The nearer to the opposing penalty area he is the more cautious defenders have to be. They are afraid to challenge for the ball in case they give away close range free kicks and penalties.

6.34 Back Flick And Turn.

Given the speed to gain a yard or two of freedom from his marker, a striker may hide the line of the ball's approach as it is played up to him. Slowing down as the ball comes near, he allows it to pass his front foot and turns his rear foot inwards to flick the ball behind his standing foot and to one side. Moving to his left, say, for a pass angled in to him he uses his left foot to flick the ball to the right. His marker will have great difficulty in changing direction to counter the flick and the striker's turn.

6.35 Split Spin.

The receiving player moves down the line of the oncoming pass encouraging his marker to be fairly close behind. As the ball arrives, the striker flicks it past and behind his opponent with the outside of one foot and spins around his opponent in the opposite direction. This technique requires a reasonable amount of space and the striker must be quick on the turn. If it achieves nothing else, a defender will be surprised by the cheek of the skill and done well it may intimidate him. He may not be quite so tight in his marking the next time, allowing the striker to turn in a more orthodox manner. It is important for strikers to keep their opponents in conditions of uncertainty.

6.36 Laying-off Passes.

The alternative to turning with the ball is to lay off passes to other players moving into supporting positions. The lay offs may be volleys, half volleys or ground passes. If a pass can be layed off at an angle to the line along which the striker and his marker are traveling, diagram 26, the marker may be deceived momentarily and the striker, having given the pass, can

Laying passes off requires a striker to be relaxed and well balanced as the ball approaches within a yard or so of his position. If he needs to clear a yard or two between him and his marker, his initial fake must be early so that he can compose himself to receive the ball and lay it off. The ball is allowed to strike his foot and it's pace is 'killed' by the relaxation of the ankle of his receiving foot. The ball is cushioned in the required direction rather than struck. If the lay-off is over ten yards or more, the foot and ankle are held firm.

All the passing and controlling skills of a high class striker are reversible.

When he seems about to pass, at the last split second a pass may be reversed into a controlling movement.

When the player looks to be certain to control the ball, a controlling movement is reversed into a pass.

Almost every technique in soccer is the exact movement opposite of another. The action is simply reversed.

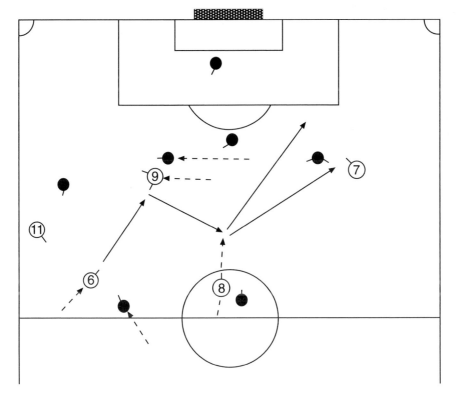

Diagram 26. *Laying passes off into areas recently vacated.*

6.4 Running With The Ball And Dribbling.

With the obvious exception of shooting, the most important skill to a striker is the ability to run and dribble the ball, often at speed and especially deceptively. Tight, dribbling control enables a striker to vary action options as circumstances change. Sudden acceleration is an invaluable asset for a striker if he can easily control and manipulate the ball as well. A striker with a tight turning circle who can run the ball directly at central defenders sets almost impossible problems. Behind them are close to goal shooting positions; positions in which defenders must be ultra cautious with their defensive methods.

To run the ball deceptively a player must learn to change control from the outside front of his foot to the inside and preferably with either foot; mastery will give him left and right directional options. Strikers don't need the exceptional trickery used by mid-field or wing players when taking on an opponent. They do need to be able to dribble or run the ball with their bodies well over the ball, occasionally shielding it; they are not trying to tempt a tackle they are trying to compel one. Often a striker will give every appearance of attacking a defense to deter them from moving forward to challenge him. He does so to fix space in front of him to enable him to set the ball up for a shot. Strikers, of all soccer players, must understand the need to use one action or threat of action to set up an alternative; the alternative is likely to be a shot at goal.

6.41 Fast Ball Running.

Running the ball at speed, the striker must be far enough away from the ball to allow him to stretch his legs into an effective sprinting stride, a stride which produces optimum speed taking into account the need for stopping, changing direction, giving and taking a return pass, avoiding a challenge, and so on.

Soccer sprinting and sprinting styles are special techniques and not those used in track sprinting.

Coaches who think that track speed (and training) transfers readily into soccer speed, if they think at all, had better think again. It doesn't.

Under threat of challenge a player will shorten his stride and reduce his speed to bring the ball within a closer playing distance. Very deceptive players, sure of their control, deliberately 'show' the ball to an opponent inviting a tackle. Having 'held back' a yard or two of acceleration, they can touch the ball away fractionally before a tackle is made. Players generally, particularly strikers, should never reveal their flat out speed until they need to.

The need, usually, involves winning a race to shoot and score.

6.42 Changing Pace.

A deceptive striker. . . and a striker who isn't deceptive has serious problems. . . seems to have effortless pace even when he hasn't!

Without electric acceleration he should learn to move as if he might have! It's called putting on the style.

Smooth acceleration from slow to fairly fast may be more deceptive than exceptional speed shown from the beginning.

For world class strikers great starting speed and change of pace, over twenty to thirty yards, are infinitely more valuable than an Olympic champion's over one hundred. Olympic sprinters would have no chance against a soccer striker. . . if each had a ball at his feet.

Even without a ball the track stars' chances might not improve where the soccer player not only started the race but decided on its direction without telling his opponents.

Different ways of increasing soccer running speed are dealt with in the chapter on specialized training.

Varying stride length while running at speed is an important attribute for a soccer player. Changing pace this way is relatively easily achieved and regular practice with and without a ball will pay enormous dividends.

Many top class soccer players are 'pigeon-toed'; their toes are turned in. This allows them to play the ball forward with the outside of each foot and with minimal interference to the sprinting stride. The ball is touched on with a forward flick of the ankle just before the foot touches the ground. The ankle is relaxed as ball contact is made. Any increase in the firmness of touch increases the distance between player and ball even at the highest speed. An Olympic sprinter's eyes are fixed firmly on the winning tape; a soccer player's search continuously far and wide for possible challenges and for action options. This enables him to adjust his movement pattern instantly to meet changing needs. Strikers who are good movers. . . and most are. . . are easy and relaxed movers.

In heavily congested areas, near to the penalty area for example, an attacker will shorten his stride and reduce the firmness with which he plays the ball forward with his front foot. He is preparing to pass, shoot, stop or change of direction.

It is important that players, young and old, practice skills with both feet. A one footed player is half a player and he presents significantly fewer problems for opponents. The ability to 'work' the ball with either foot opens up a vastly increased range of options, no more so than when stopping, starting and changing direction.

6.43 Stopping, Starting and Changing Direction.

The ball can be 'worked' with the inside of the foot, the outside of the foot, the sole of the foot and the heel.

When dribbling with the inside of the right foot, the ball will be most easily stopped with the inside of the left and vice versa. When a striker is running with the ball immediately in front of him, he will be able to stop the ball most easily by using the sole (the under surface) of his foot. He literally puts his foot on the ball. Clever players can, in the same movement, pull the ball backwards with the sole of the foot: very useful in evading sliding tacklers. Alternatively he can pass his foot forward and over the ball to stop it with his heel.

Any more elaborate ways of stopping with the ball may not warrant the time needed to master them. With no more than a slightly exaggerated stopping action, each of the above methods can be used to stop and move the ball in the opposite direction in one movement. Occasionally, stopping with the ball is not enough to deceive an opponent. If, in anticipation of the stop, he commits himself to a flying tackle, it will be necessary to move body and ball out of his way. . . and quickly.

It's not possible to over-emphasize the importance of always having a reserve action option.

Stopping and starting skills are complementary. Stop the ball with the inside of the left foot and it will be easiest to start with the inside of the right and so on. Changing direction may be achieved with or without a 'faked' move to deceive opponents. The suddenness of the change is likely to be deceptive enough.

If a feint (faked) move is used, the player will move his foot towards or over the ball as if to play it. The feint will only be effective if it is made to seem a natural part of a full technique. Elaborate exaggeration only deceives poor players.

6.44 Body Swerve.

To produce the impression of swerve, the player makes as if to move off, to his right say, with the ball on his left foot. At the last moment instead of playing the ball to the right with his left foot, his foot passes over or behind the ball. His body language telegraphs his intention to move right decisively. Having passed his foot over the ball (or behind it), the striker flicks the ball left with the outside of his left foot and moves left, leaving his opponent over-balanced in the opposite direction.

'Feint one way and go the other' is the basis of tricky dribbling and the better the 'acting' the more successful the deception.

Defenders will make their challenge to tackle but may also try to follow through to shoulder the striker off the ball. . . fairly or otherwise. The striker will move the ball just far enough away from the tackle to avoid it. At same time he sways the whole of his body above the hips clear of any attempt to charge or body block him. Great players using this skill seem almost to defy the laws of gravity as they swerve away from opponents.

6.45 Dribbling With The 'Inside' Foot.

The 'inside' foot, as different from the inside OF the foot, is the foot nearer to an opponent. Inside foot dribbling allows the striker to take the ball much nearer to an opponent before swerving past him. An attacker often deliberately 'shows' his opponent the ball to tempt a tackle. Obviously a defender will fancy his chance of winning the ball where he doesn't have to stretch across the striker to tackle for it.

Inside foot dribbling is of special advantage to a wide attacker who, having shown an opponent the ball, can swerve past him on his outside and be able to cross the ball or to shoot without adjusting his stride.

A left winger's inside foot will, of course, be his right foot and vice versa for the opposite winger.

If the attacker can shoot or cross the ball with either foot the problem for a defender becomes considerable. He has difficulty in preventing a good cross pass following an outside 'break'. . . a quick movement past him on the defender's outside. . . and if he positions himself to block the outside break, he leaves room for the attacker to move inside to shoot. Attackers must learn to play off both feet. A living legend of English football, Bobby Charlton, could do so with elegance and breathtaking acceleration. Pelé of Brazil had unstoppable power and poise in moving 'both ways'. Maradonna, the Argentinian, World Number One in his time, was exceptionally strong and dangerously deceptive off both feet.

6.46 Dribbling With The 'Outside' Foot.

Some coaches place great emphasis on the need, as they see it, for attackers to be able to touch, tap and stroke the ball with every part of each foot in order to perfect some sort of ball mastery. This is unrealistic and is not the kind of perceptive skill required by great soccer players.

Ball juggling skills, whether in the air or on the ground, may appear to be relevant to soccer's needs, unfortunately they aren't.

As Nikita Simonyan, then the head coach in the USSR and himself a skillful international player, said to me during World Cup '78, in Argentina. . . at the time we were watching the ball juggling virtuosity of The Coca-Cola kids. . . "Very interesting, very good. . . for a circus!"

Soccer skills must be learned and practiced in controlled, competitive situations specially devised to represent the demands of the game.

The ability to devise and manipulate effective practice situations is the difference between a real coach and a trainer.

The successful dribblers in soccer have mastered at most two or three 'tricks'. The problem for a defender is not WHAT an attacker will do to deceive him, it's WHEN he will do it. Every full back in world soccer knew what the dribbling maestro, Stanley Matthews, would do to beat him.

He moved towards his opponent slowly, tapping the ball from one foot to the other, his body swaying to right and left almost hypnotically. When his opponent was off balance Matthews flicked the ball to the right. . . always to the right. . . with the outside of his right foot and he was gone! Andy Beattie, a Scottish international defender of world class, seriously thought that Matthews hypnotized defenders, himself included, with his ball tapping and swaying movements.

The key to Matthews's success was his patience in waiting until the defender tried to tackle. Then Matthews made his outside break with the speed and balance of a striking cobra.

Stanley Matthews's close control at high speed, his wonderful delicacy of touch in either foot together with a super sense of balance. . . or rather unbalance. . . in opponents, was astonishing. Even more astonishing was the fact that he retained his skill at making an outside break and out sprinting international class defenders until well past his fortieth year.

Garrincha of Brazil had the same mesmerizing skill but where Matthews used dribbling skill to create team scoring opportunities, Garrincha often tormented defenders for the sake of demoralizing them. Not a bad idea at that!

An 'outside' dribbler usually threatens to attack inside the opponent's position before breaking outside. If the defender allows the threatened inside break to succeed, as we have seen, it may lead to a shot on goal, if the attacking player is two footed!! A defender's fundamental responsibility is to prevent shots on goal. But in positioning himself to block an inside move, the defender leaves himself open on the outside.

6.47 Screening And Dribbling.
Where a striker cannot make an effective dribbling or passing move, he may have to screen (hide) the ball to keep possession until opportunity presents itself. Screening the ball involves using his outside foot to 'work' the ball while hiding it behind his body. Twisting and turning will be necessary against a determined opponent and the outside foot may be left or right according to the challenge of the opponent.

Using constantly changing body movements to deceive his opponent, the attacker waits until the opponent makes a positive move to tackle down one side or the other. The attacker then turns his opponent, using his body to protect the ball and moves off at speed.

Screening becomes illegal obstruction when the dribbler leaves the ball and uses his body as a barrier unfairly to prevent the opponent from challenging for it.

6.5 Dribbling Principles.
Essentially, dribbling involves the following simple principles.

6.51 Creating False Impressions.
The striker 'shows' defenders his intention to move the ball one way when his real intention is quite different.

Trickery when dribbling is a matter of opposites. Before moving quickly a player slows down or pretends to stop. Before stopping, a player creates an impression that he is about to accelerate.

If he intends to move right, he creates the impression that he will go left. If he intends to dribble, he creates the impression that he will pass . . . and so on.

6.52 'Showing' The Ball.
The dribbling player will show an opponent enough of the ball to tempt him into a tackle; he is confident that he can move the ball before the

defender completes his challenge. Great dribblers are great tempters, at their most dangerous when they seem to be least secure. They create the impression that the ball is not under perfect control when it is. Dribbling at high speed, Maradonna often seemed about to fall flat on his face. . . but never did.

6.53 Faking.

The attacker uses 'fake' (false) moves with his eyes, head, body and feet . . . and sometimes his voice. . . to disconcert and deceive the defender. Falsifying body language is vital to top flight players.

Clever players use their eyes to present defenders with false information about their intentions. They look into the distance as if searching for an opportunity to pass when they intend to dribble. A look and shout to a teammate (who isn't there!) behind the defender gives a false impression of support when there isn't any.

Great players are great 'con' men.

6.54 Unbalancing An Opponent.

Patience must be used to 'work' the defender to break his concentration. Having unbalanced an opponent (sent him the wrong way), the striker needs the starting thrust and acceleration to leave him for dead.

Lack of balance occurs for a split second, during which the dribbling player must explode into decisive action. He sets himself without appearing to do so.

Many talented dribblers appear unprepared and without confidence when the opposite is really the case.

Chapter 7
Training and Practice

Time for training and practice is valuable. Routines must be realistic to enable a striker to fulfill his role effectively. Practice must be 'tailor made' and progressive to make him a better player.

From time to time it will be necessary for a player to practice skills which he has already mastered.

Learning new skills is based upon increasing the confidence in known skills.

As players mature, practice of familiar skills should not need regular coach supervision. Players unwilling to practice seriously, often without the presence of a coach, are unlikely to become exceptional players.

Older players will be more concerned with maintaining the range of their skills, together with the levels of fitness needed to sustain them.

Some players, however, continue to improve their skills, in quality and in range, almost to the ends of their careers; others hardly improve at all after their mid-twenties. It's all in the mind, either a player wants to improve or he doesn't: in which case he won't!

Young players are driven by unfulfilled ambitions. Most are hungry for new skills; physical conditioning will come second to skills practice although some practices can be adapted in intensity to affect certain physical conditioning (training) objectives.

The younger the player the more general his physical training: the older the player, the more specific it must become.

From the earliest age possible, all children, whatever their sporting inclinations, must be encouraged to run, skip, hop and jump. . . especially run. And for would be soccer stars, run with a ball.

Most running should involve some sprinting. Outstanding ability in any athletic sport is rarely possible without exceptional 'wheels and engines', legs and lungs if you like. The foundations for strong, fast legs and a powerful 'engine' (heart and lungs) are laid down much nearer to three years of age than to thirteen!

'Keep Kids Clear Of Cars'.

That should be a motto deeply imprinted in the minds of everyone connected with young soccer players. Car riding spells the death of athletic ambition.

Players' early years should involve them in a great deal of ball play and almost as much running, preferably both at the same time. Why run without a ball when it is almost as easy to run with one. . . everywhere?

How much is a great deal? World class players of my certain knowledge remember spending six hours a day or more at soccer play and practice.

Much of this time was spent practicing with a ball, in most cases a tennis ball, and not a coach in sight.

Coaches can tell players what they should be doing and how they should be doing it. They can show players how best to practice and to train: they cannot do it for them!

7.1 Personal Practice.

A striker's personal practice routines should concentrate on the following:

7.11 Close dribbling leading to shots on goal, or at a target, using both feet.

7.12 Instant control when receiving the ball leading to a tight turn, a dribble and shot or fake shot.

7.13 First touch shooting to hit targets, with either foot.

7.14 One and two touch interpassing moves, involving one or two additional players leading to shots on target.

7.15 Diving and jumping headers to hit targets.

Targets will be small or full size goals or even marks on walls.

Mastery of these techniques is vital. Practice routines are set out later in this chapter.

Strikers' Practices.

The following are proven, effective practices which will be valuable to all players and which can be used without a coach in sight. Nevertheless coaches can use the same practices as the foundation of their practice and coaching programs. Space and distances can be adjusted for different ages and levels of skill.

(A) Close Dribbling To Shoot.
1 v 1 practice.

Place two markers eight yards (or less) apart to represent goals. Set up two such goals on a practice area thirty yards long and ten yards wide.

The thirty yard long pitch is marked out in three ten yard zones.

An end zone is a defensive or shooting zone.

Each of two practicing players, in turn, dribbles the ball at his opponent trying to gain access to that player's end zone.

A player can score only in his opponent's end zone.

If the defending player tackles for the ball successfully he can score by dribbling (not shooting) the ball over the other player's goal line and within the goal.

A goal resulting from a tackle does not affect the 'in turn' sequence of dribbling and scoring attempts.

Both players are 'live' all the time.

This practice is very demanding. Increase the players to two at each end. After each 1 v 1 contest and a resulting 'goal' or shot at goal, the second player from that end replaces the player who finished off the last attack. That player retires to the behind goal position. Scores are added up over the full practice period.

The moment when a striker loses the ball is when he should try hardest to get it back.

Scoring can be made more difficult by placing two additional markers two yards behind the goal markers, diagram 27. These represent side netting areas: shots aimed there are much more likely to beat the goalkeeper.

A score in the 'side netting' counts three points; a goal scored within the normal area scores one point.

All skill practice areas are prepared on a space allowance of roughly 200 square yards per player: slightly less if practice is needed to develop skill in 'tight' areas e.g. close to goal.

For very young players, 5 - 7 years, the space allowance may drop to 100 square yards per player.

Where practice grids are set up they are based upon so many 10 yds. x 10 yds 'boxes': obviously 1 box produces 100 square yards of space and each player needs a maximum of 2 boxes i.e. 200 square yards. 8 boxes produce 800 square yards of space, enough for a 4 player practice and so on.

A practice 'grid' (a large number of boxes) equal to one half of a good size pitch, 80 yds. wide x 60 yds. long say, produces possibilities for setting up any number of smaller practice areas and used to the full is also suitable for 'phase' practice involving two full teams on attack or defense.

(B) Continuous Dribbling and Shooting (advanced).

    Players: 2 groups of 3, working in 1 v 2 situations
    Area :   40 yds. x 10.
    Goals: 2 mini goals, each 2 - 3 yds apart, at both ends of the
                practice grid.

Diagram 28, A attacks. B cannot challenge until A enters his box.

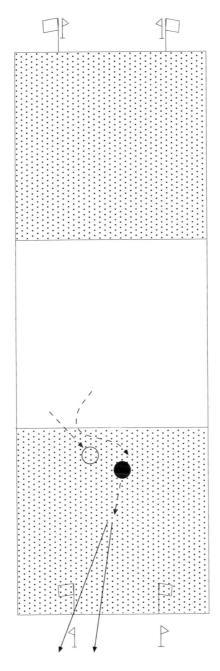

Diagram 27. *1 v 1 dribbling and shooting practice.*

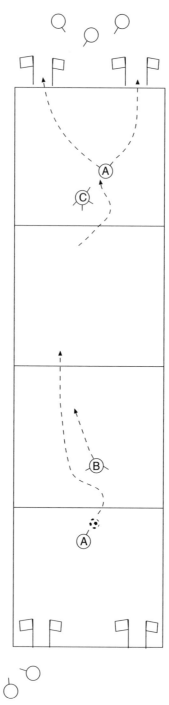

Diagram 28. *Advanced dribbling practice.*

When A has dribbled past B he has a free box before entering the end zone where he is challenged by C.

A dribbling player can score by dribbling (3 points) the ball through one of the mini goals or by passing (1 point) the ball through it.

If A loses the ball an opponent tries to dribble the ball into one of the goals at the opposite end. A recovers to regain possession or prevent a goal.

On completion of one attack, all players move down one square. An attack starts from each end in turn.

Two or even three groups can work in turn: two groups rest while one works.

Two defenders against one attacker is a difficult but realistic practice for mature players. With sensible coaching a player learns to take advantage of the slightest opportunity to beat or even half beat opponents to shoot.

Dribbling options are increased when defenders are unsure when a shot is likely. When set to block a shot they are more likely to be beaten by a dribbling run. Keeping opponents guessing is the difference between a match winning striker and an honest. . . but unsuccessful 'trier'.

C) Diagram 29. As practice success indicates the need for more complex situations, the numbers can be increased e.g. to 2 attackers v 3 defenders. The practice area will be enlarged accordingly e.g for 5 players, 1,000 sq. yds. of space i.e. 50 yds x 20.

The practice area is divided into three zones, two end zones each 15 yards deep and one mid zone, 20 yards deep.

Inter-passing is allowed only in the mid zone.

The sweeper, 'S', can only leave his end zone when he has challenged an opponent for the ball successfully at which time he can dribble out of his end zone to set up a 3 v 2 situation in the mid zone.

Only an attacker with the ball can enter the end zone where he tries to beat S and run the ball through either of the two goals.

Practice is continuous. If it is found to be too demanding physically, another two pairs can wait at either end and each 'match' will last for a fixed period of three to five minutes.

(D) 'Conditioned' Practice.

Practice in small groups or in any form of the game is especially effective when the playing options of players are governed by a special rule or 'condition'.

Conditioned practice must not be confused with 'conditioning' i.e. physical training.

Examples of game 'conditions' to govern dribbling and shooting

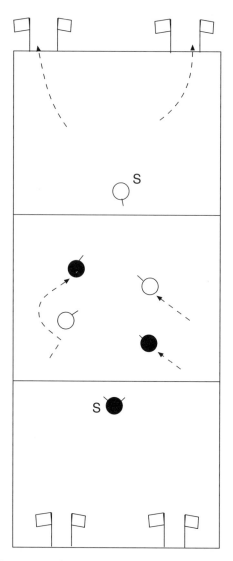

Diagram 29. *Small team practice conditioned to emphasize individual dribbling skills.*

practices for strikers are:

    (a) Dribble only with your right (or left) foot, shoot with either.

    (b) Shoot only with your right (left) foot, dribble with either.

    (c) Touch the ball at least 5 times before shooting or passing.

    (d) Play the ball from your right foot to your left and back before attempting a shot and vice versa.

    (e) Whatever the basic practice, score two bonus points each time you play the ball through your opponent's legs and regain possession of the ball behind him.

(f) Before trying to dribble past an opponent hide the ball by turning your back to him.

Other conditions can be invented to meet the needs of any coaching or practice aim. A player can impose 'conditions' on his own play without telling anyone else. All great players do this to exert discipline on their practice.

Playing with a ball for fun may be pleasant but it isn't practice. Without targets to aim for, which 'conditions' provide, players have no way of knowing if practice is paying off.

(E) Turning To Shoot Or To Dribble And Shoot.

In a six box grid, diagram 30, there are three mini goals, each goal two or three yards wide, at each end. The feeders must remain in the box in which they start the practice.

Players white 4 and 6 interpass, choosing when to pass forward to strikers white 8 or 9. These strikers try to turn to shoot first time or to dribble and shoot or to dribble.

Later the two mid zone players will be opposed in a 2 v 1 situation. Making their play more realistic makes the play of the striker also more realistic.

A scoring shot through any of the three goals scores 2 points but if a player can turn and dribble the ball through one of the three goals he scores 10 points. Strikers in the forward zone can play the ball back to the mid zone players to gain a rest or to set up another attack if they wish. At the completion of an attack or if a defender tackles for the ball successfully, the ball is returned to the mid zone where the players turn and repeat the practice at the other end.

As shooting improves, goal defenders can be introduced to defend all three goals; initially without the use of hands, later with their use.

If an attacker is completely unsuccessful in turning off his marker, the marker should be left out of the practice or his options should be significantly restricted.

The striker should practice one, at most two, specific turning skills. Having tried out the moves unopposed, or against token opposition, successfully, the pressure of opposition to the striker is gradually increased by progressively removing the restrictions imposed on the defender. As the striker develops confidence in using his turning, dribbling and shooting skills, so opposition pressure is gradually increased but never to a level at which he fails.

Skill learning must be based upon success in practice. Practice in which a player fails more often than he succeeds, or which ends with failure, will

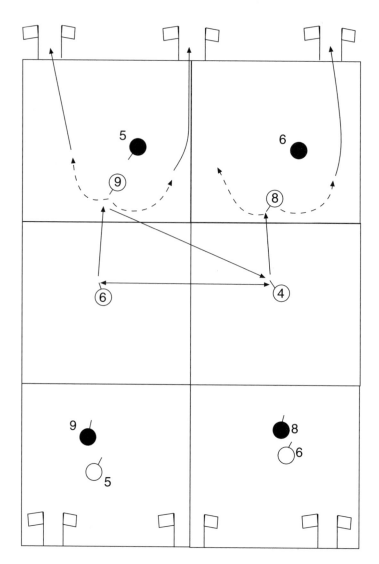

Diagram 30. *Turning to shoot or dribble and shoot.*

only improve a player's skill at failing.

Even in kick-about practices, players must look for opportunities for using new moves, successfully or otherwise.

When practicing alone, a player must imagine that he is actually playing in real soccer situations; he must fantasize about success.

Trial and success not trial and error is the surest path to soccer skill. Players remember successful practice and forget failure. . . quickly!

'Odd Man In' Practice.

The realism of practice is not significantly reduced when the group upon which practice is focused has the advantage of an extra player: sometimes a number of extra players.

If the practice group contains an even number of players, the 'odd man' (extra player) can be created by imposing a 'condition'. e.g. In possession of the ball **ALL** players join in the attack. Without possession, one player in the team **MUST** drop back onto the goal line. He becomes the 'handling' defender. It doesn't have to be the same player who drops back each time.

This condition ensures that the attacking side has an extra attacker.

If the practice objective is defensive, the condition can be reversed. i.e. in possession of the ball, two players must remain on their team's goal line. This allows the opposing team to have a goalkeeper and one extra outfield defender.

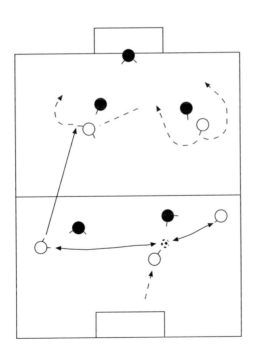

Diagram 31. *Turning with the ball to dribble or shoot inside a penalty area. Alternatively shooting from outside the penalty area.*

F) Shooting And Dribbling In And Near The Penalty Area.

The practice area is made up of two approximate penalty areas. For convenience let's say that a penalty area is 40 yards wide and 20 yards deep. i.e. eight practice 'boxes', each 10 yards x 10 yards. Two penalty areas will take up 16 boxes. Diagram 31. 16 boxes provide practice space for 8 or 10 players. Remember, penalty area practice means that players have to become accustomed to less space than they might enjoy in less dangerous parts of the pitch.

In diagram 31, each 'team' has a goalkeeper, two strikers and two supporting attackers.

Practice 'Conditions'.

(1) The two strikers remain inside their opponents' penalty area all the time.

(2) The supporting players cannot join them.

(3) The goalkeeper of the team in possession can operate as an extra supporting player.

(4) The defending team's goalkeeper must always be on his goal line except when saving shots.

(5) If close range shooting is the objective: shots may be attempted only by the two players in the forward area.

(6) If long range shooting is the objective: shots cannot be taken within the forward area.

(7) The ball may be passed or dribbled in any direction.

The number of attackers in the forward area can be varied to suit the practice emphasis.

This practice situation can be adapted to produce any manner of attacking tactical ideas except realistic crossing opportunities.

(G) Crossing And Shooting.

Extend the two penalty areas to include the full width of a pitch.
Diagram 32. Each attack can now involve wingers and the possibilities of crosses from wide attacking positions into the penalty area.

Initially any attacker moving into a wide channel cannot be followed by an opponent. This enables him to concentrate on crossing the ball accurately. As practice proceeds the coach may allow one opponent to move wide to challenge the wide attacker.

The extended practice area can take in a number of extra players.

Working on a ratio of 1 player to 200 square yards, we can use 8

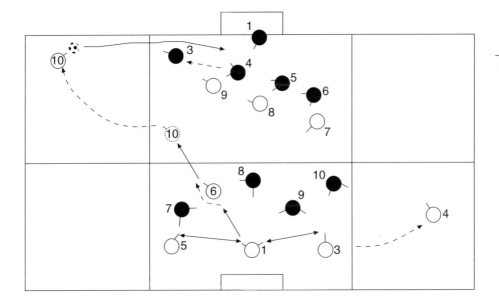

Diagram 32. *Turning, dribbling, crossing and shooting in two expanded penalty areas. Repetition functional practice.*

outfield players in 4 v 4 situations in each practice 'half'. The goalkeeper can be used to give a team in possession of the ball a one player advantage where it is needed to ensure that practice is successful more often than not.

This is repeated functional practice wherein players are coached to perform as they would in the game in similar circumstances.

Strikers must be adaptable. To produce shooting chances for each other each must know what the other (or others) are most likely to do in most situations. Strikers become very dangerous when opponents feel sure that they know what the strikers will do in any given situation. Skillful strikers encourage them to think that way. . . before springing a surprise move.

Success in doing something out of the ordinary depends upon persuading opponents that they know what to expect.

(H) Pressure Practice; Instant Shooting.
To get in an instant shot the striker must make space for himself to shoot or he must get to the ball before any opponent. The techniques used we have dealt with earlier.

In a four box grid, diagram 33, a goal is at one end of the grid.

Initially goalkeeper E stands behind the goals: waiting strikers act as ball retrievers, R.

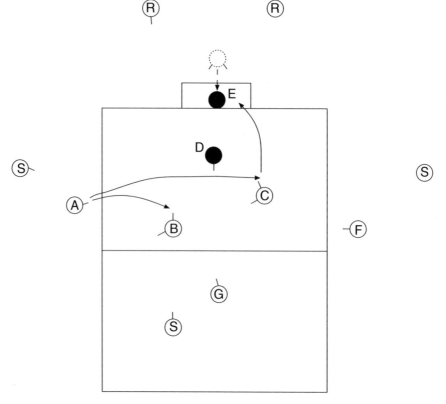

Diagram 33: *Pressure practice.*

There are three service players, A, F and G, with three or four balls each.

Player A serves to B, or C, who controls and shoots or passes to C, or B, who shoots first time. Only the first receiver can control the ball before shooting or passing.

The serving sequence always is counter-clockwise i.e. A to G to F to A.

Defender, D, is positioned between the strikers B and C and the goal; to begin with he does not interfere.

E cannot act as a goalkeeper until the strikers are making accurate shots on goal. Establishing the confidence of practicing players at each stage of practice development is of paramount importance.

As confidence grows with success, the defenders are:

(1) allowed to block the shot but not prevent the player from shooting

(2) allowed to challenge the striker as he shoots.

Practice can be intensified by speeding up the service of the ball to the strikers. Where the aim is to improve a player's skill, pressure should never be allowed to cause his skill to deteriorate. Accuracy and control are everything to a soccer marksman.

Following practice success the situation in the shooting box may become 4 v 2 or even with very skillful players 3 v 2. The strikers always have the advantage numerically. If pressure practice needs to be focused on a specific aspect of one player's shooting techniques the servers need only adjust their services to achieve the required focus.

(I) All Action Shooting
The pitch is a twelve box practice area. The shooting game involves 3 v 3 in each of the two half pitches. One 'floating' player always plays for the team which has the ball and he alone may move freely about the whole practice area.

Practice Conditions.
(1) The four groups remain in their respective halves of the pitch.
(2) The floater can move about freely.

All the groups are both attackers and defenders, they attack to shoot and score whenever the ball is in their half. When a goal is scored or a shot is taken which misses, the goalkeeper at that end puts the ball back into play by kicking or throwing it into the other half of the area.

(3) A shot on target saved counts for one point. A scoring shot counts for three points. A shot which misses the goal earns a deduction of two points.

Different 'conditions', i.e. special rules, can be imposed to emphasize different practice aims. e.g. 'Pass, follow your pass and shoot' makes players think of taking positive action as soon as they have passed, in this case they move to support the pass receiver.

Interpassing moves in and close to the penalty area, through the element of surprise, can be remarkably effective in producing good shooting chances. If attackers are prepared to run the ball at their nearest opponent rather than to pass it to probe for an opening, those opponents may be shocked into careless challenges or even into making no sort of positive challenges at all.

'Run the ball at your nearest opponent' in the practice game described earlier means that the floater has to make a positive move with the ball thereby allowing other attackers to make space for him or to offer themselves as interpassing options to create shooting chances.

A 'Pass and move across the shooting area' condition helps strikers to be aware of the need to 'draw' defenders away from central and therefore important shooting areas.

(J) Diving and Jumping Headers.
The key to success with scoring headers is to deliver the ball so that strikers can run to jump to attack it, not to the area in which they are standing.

The temptation always is to cross the ball trying to find the heads of certain players, usually the best jumpers. Players who are compelled to make standing jumps to head or to use very short runs to take off, cannot jump as high or as positively as those who attack it off say a ten yard run.

It is important that attackers keep well away from the target areas for crosses and attack them as late and therefore as powerfully as possible.

7.2 Training.

7.21 Speed Agility.
Strikers need to accelerate to high speed from a standing or slow moving start over short distances, ten to thirty yards at most. They also need the agility to change from a high speed sprint, with or without the ball, to a sudden stop, a change of direction, to receive or give a pass, to head or shoot for goal.

7.22 Speed Endurance.
This is the capacity for making many runs with and without a ball, at fast to moderate speed, while occasionally making short, very fast runs.

In a match where the striker's team is under pressure for long periods, against a much superior team for example, a striker will offer himself as a relief outlet for his severely tested defenders. This will need constant movement across the field, as the ball is transferred to different attacking points by his opponents. The striker's movements will offer temporary outlets should his own defenders manage to play the ball out of defense. His alternative is to calculate the chances of making a counter attack by himself supported, if at all, by one other player. A team having a striker with speed superior to that of any opposing defender, may prefer him to preserve that speed by keeping his endurance testing work to a minimum. Even against heavy odds, the special attributes of one player, used sparingly and cleverly, can swing a game: even the most one-sided of them. That is what tactics are all about: making the most of what you've got.

7.23 Power Agility.

Agility is the ability to change position on the field over short distances at optimum speed while using the skills of the game. Agility is also the capacity for changing the shape of the body at speed while using the game's skills. Most obviously the second form of agility is particularly needed by goalkeepers whose performances are more gymnastic than athletic.

Power is the capacity for overcoming resistance at speed.

Power agility is needed to win races over short distances from standing starts, often with stops, starts and changes of direction and usually employing a game skill before, during or after the run. It is also needed to jump to head or to save a shot, often against resistance offered by opponents. . . not all of it legal.

A basic pre-requisite for improving power is an improvement in strength.

7.24 Strength.

This is not the primary strength of the weight lifter. It is the applied strength used by a player to kick a ball as hard as circumstances allow. It is the strength needed to resist attempts by opponents to knock a striker off the ball fairly or otherwise. . . more often than not, otherwise.

Without strength, gaining the power necessary for success in top class soccer is not really possible.

7.25 Suppleness.

Suppleness, sometimes referred to as flexibility, is the capacity for stretching, bending, twisting the various joint complexes which enable us to move in different ways, some of them barely imaginable, as required by the high speed, athletic, gymnastic game which is soccer.

A striker may have to contort his limbs desperately beyond reasonable limits to reach the ball to score. He must twist and turn, sometimes violently, to evade opponents and to get to the ball first.

The normal requirements of daily movement are far exceeded in sport and none more so than in soccer. Goalkeepers are special in the sense that their responsibilities and special skills place extraordinary demands on their bones, ligaments tendons and muscles. As I have said, they are soccer's gymnasts and their practice and training routines will reflect their unique requirements. Soccer strikers, with whom goalkeepers frequently come into conflict, have similar if not quite the same needs for flexibility. They need most of the goalkeeper's agility skills exercised in much the same way but without the allowance of using their hands.

Conclusion

To be effective, practice and training must be planned; they must be purposeful and progressive. Some people believe that practice can be play. It can't. In the context of soccer, practice and play are contradictory terms. Play is spontaneous and unpredictable. Practice and training, on the other hand, are pre-determined and objective. They set out to achieve specific objectives which should be measurable. Practice which does not allow both player and coach to measure the change in performance which the practice has been designed to bring about really isn't practice at all.

Nevertheless, the reference point for all soccer practice and training must be in-game performance. And there must be no doubt about an order of priority, training must be subordinate to skill. In fact training which doesn't relate directly to skill improvement may not be worth the indulgence.

Some young players the world over become extraordinarily skillful at juggling or dribbling a soccer ball. They develop these astonishing levels of technical mastery over a ball through hours and hours of ball practice.

And for improving their soccer skill it's a waste of valuable time!

Juggling or dribbling a soccer ball when no other player is likely to interfere with a player's skill is one thing, to exercise the same skill when one or more opponents are doing their utmost to prevent success is another ball game. . . in this case, literally.

To be effective in improving a player's game performance, skill practice must be realistic; realism is produced when teammates and opponents are involved in the practice in a realistic way.

Of course soccer skills do involve the different techniques which make up the game and players need to achieve certain levels of competence while they are learning the game.

The emphasis must be on while they are learning to play the game. The striker's technical skills are learned and refined in the game and it is the game itself which shows a player and his coach what he needs to know and to practice.

Other books from **REEDSWAIN**

Allen Wade's NEW Books and others in this series.

PRINCIPLES OF
Effective Coaching
#245 • $14.95

TEACHING THE
Principles of Soccer
#148 • $14.95

POSITIONAL PLAY
Midfield
#2532 • $12.95

POSITIONAL PLAY
Back Defenders
#2531 • $12.95

POSITIONAL PLAY
Goalkeeping
#2534 • $12.95

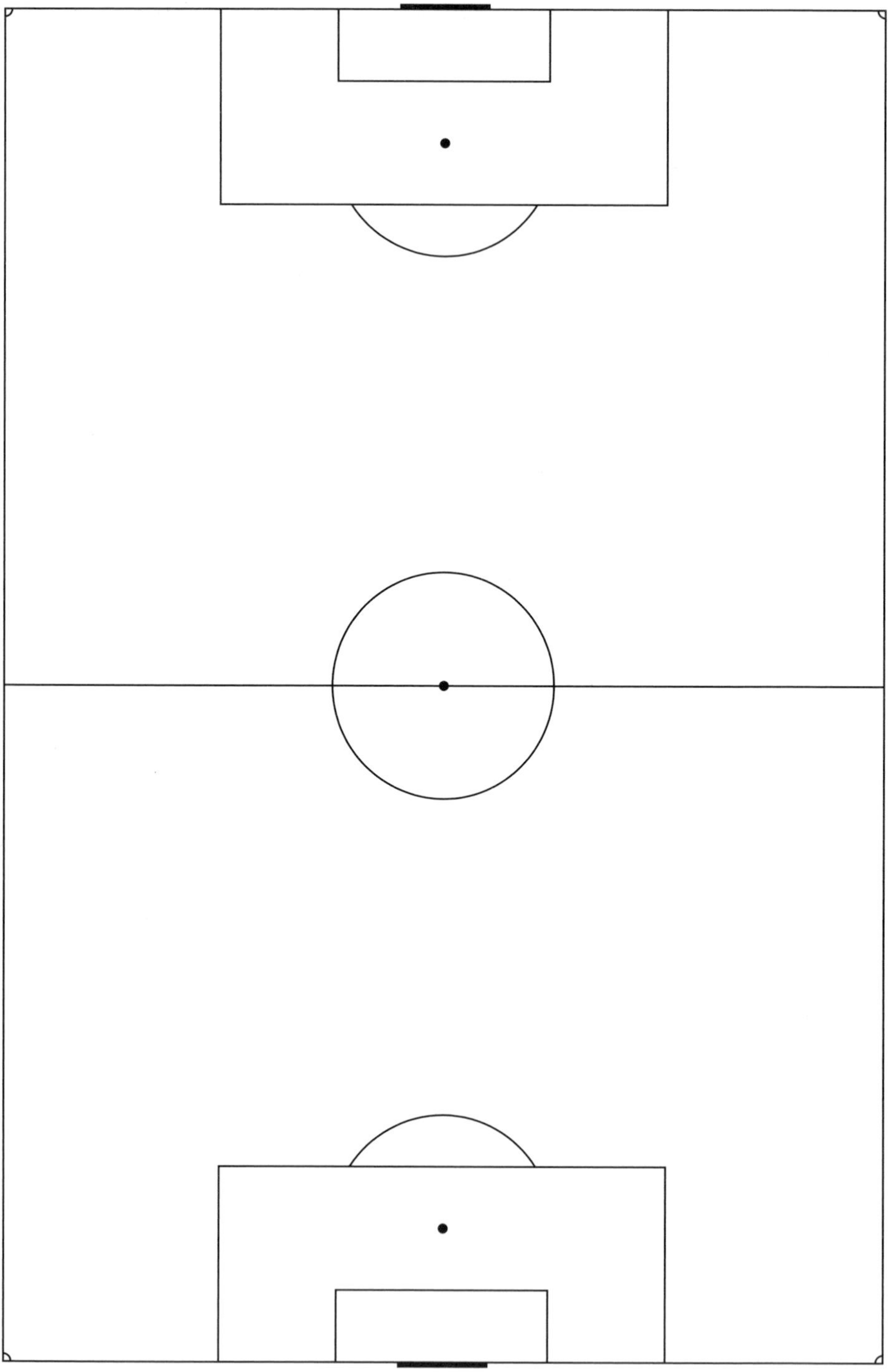

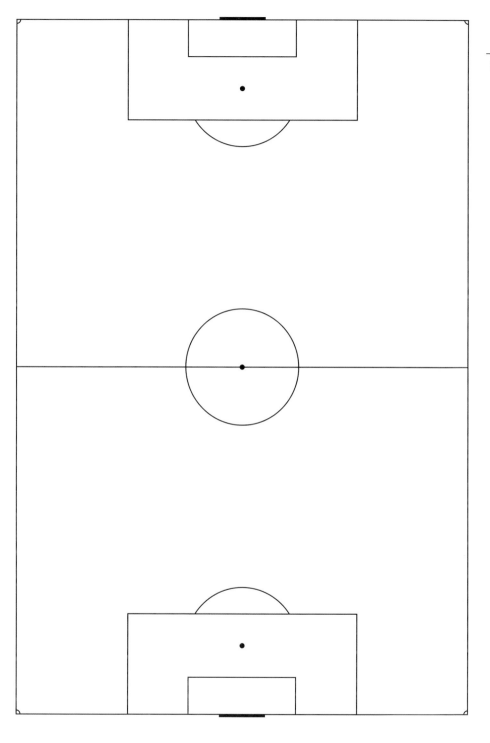

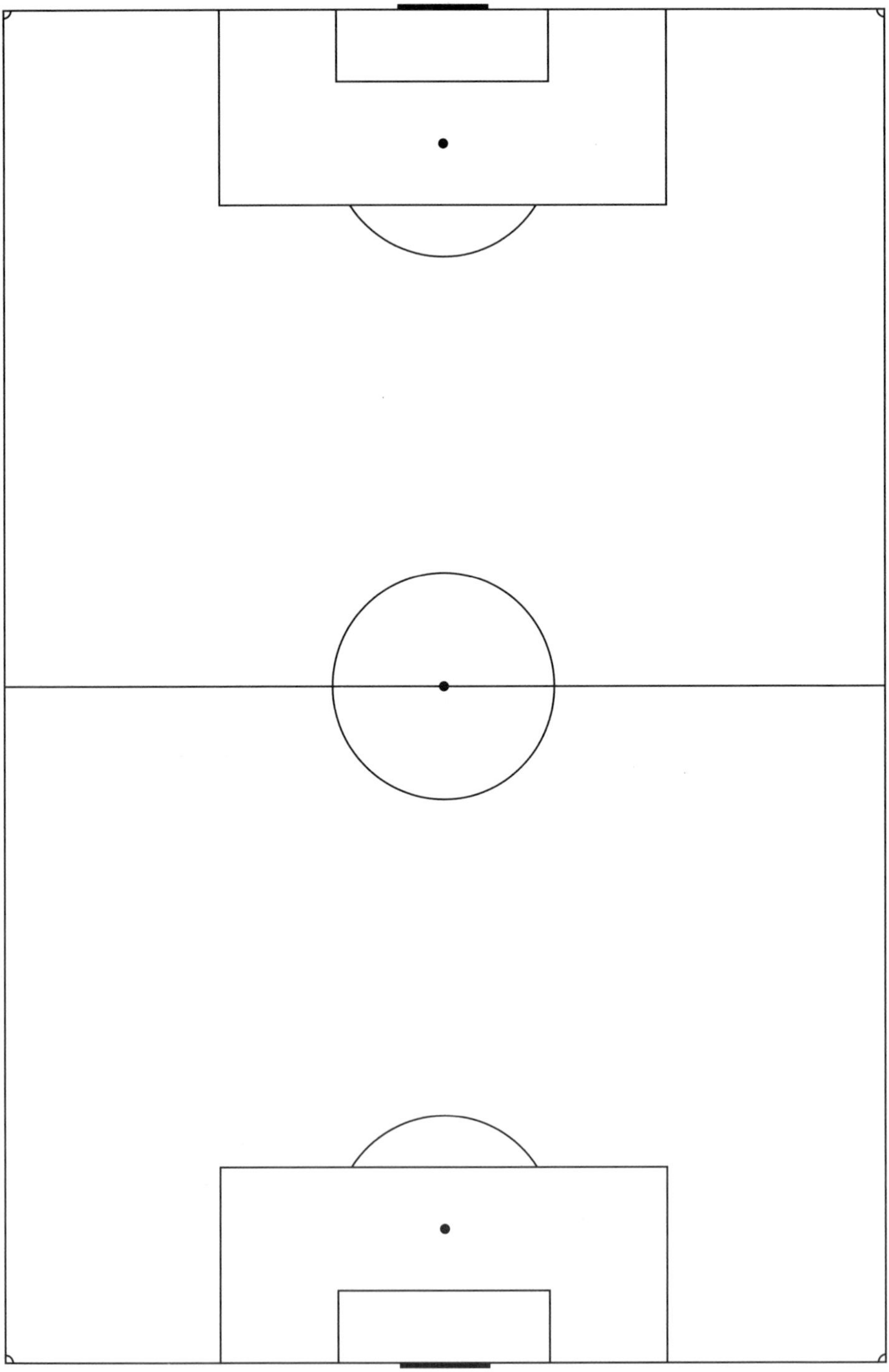

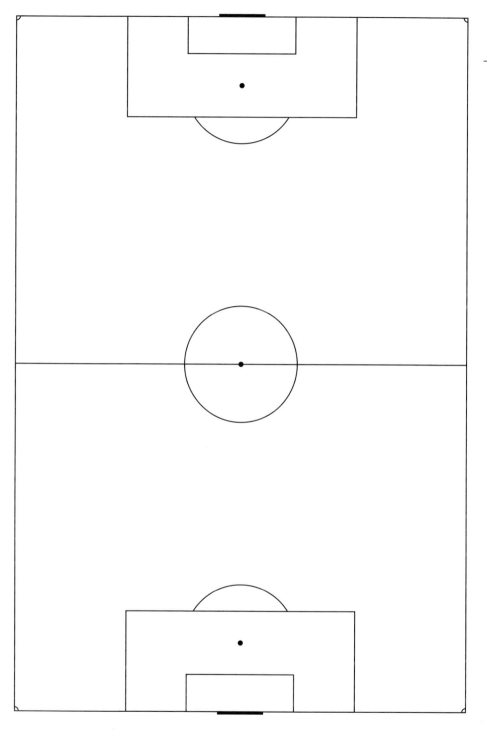

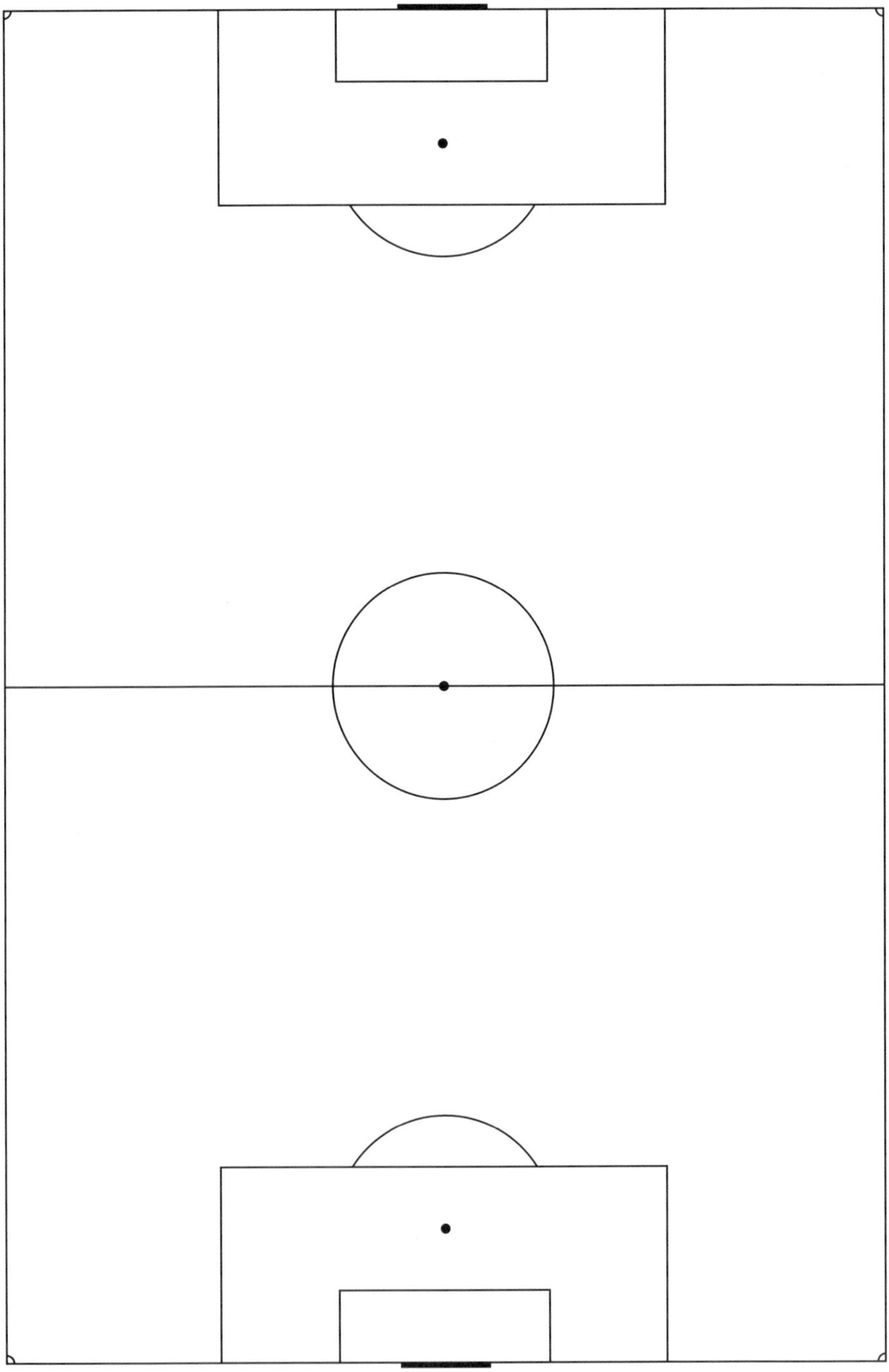